"Along with overhunting and habitat destruction, introduced species are one of the mindless horsemen of the environmental apocalypse. Landers uses the tools of the hunter to battle the scourge of invaders — from giant Canada geese to swamp rats, or nutria — across the country."

— JOE ROMAN, EDITOR 'N' CHEF OF THE WEBSITE EAT THE INVADERS AND AUTHOR OF *LISTED: DISPATCHES FROM AMERICA'S ENDANGERED SPECIES ACT*

"*Eating Aliens* shows how eating our way out of the invasive species issue can be a delicious challenge well worth the undertaking."

— SARAH SWENTY, MANAGING EDITOR, *COOKING WILD* MAGAZINE

"Let Jackson Landers teach you how to eat in a fun, exotic, delicious, and nutritious way that can also help restore the environment!"

— CHEF BUN LAI, MIYA'S SUSHI

"Grab your shotgun and your frying pan, and let *Eating Aliens* be your guide to becoming the ultimate invasivore!"

— MATTHEW WEINGARTEN, CHEF AND AUTHOR OF *PRESERVING WILD FOODS*

EATING ALIENS

EATING ALIENS

One Man's Adventures Hunting Invasive Animal Species

Jackson Landers

FOREWORD BY **HANK SHAW**

ILLUSTRATIONS BY TAVIS COBURN

Storey Publishing

The mission of Storey Publishing is to serve our customers by publishing practical information that encourages personal independence in harmony with the environment.

Edited by Carleen Madigan
Art direction and book design by Alethea Morrison
Illustrations by © Tavis Coburn

Storey books are available for special premium and promotional uses and for customized editions. For further information, please call 1-800-793-9396.

Storey Publishing
210 MASS MoCA Way
North Adams, MA 01247
www.storey.com

Printed in United States by Edwards Brothers Malloy
10 9 8 7 6 5 4 3 2 1

Storey Publishing is committed to making environmentally responsible manufacturing decisions. This book was printed in the United States on paper made from sustainably harvested fiber.

Library of Congress Cataloging-in-Publication Data

Landers, Jackson.
Eating aliens / by Jackson Landers.
p. cm.
1. Hunting—Anecdotes. 2. Hunting stories. I. Title.
SK33.L327 2012
639'.1—dc23
2012017449

"Nature is all very well in her place, but she must not be allowed to make things untidy."

STELLA GIBBONS, *COLD COMFORT FARM*

Contents

Foreword

WE HUMANS ARE DESIGNED TO EAT A LITTLE OF A LOT, not a lot of a little. For as long as we've been human — which is far longer than we have been herders or tillers of the soil — a diverse diet has been our best ally against the slings and arrows of disease, famine, and hardship. It is our ability to fully enjoy nature's buffet that has made us so strong as a species.

So why do we now choose to limit ourselves to a handful of foods? The reasons are many, but most center on our almost complete divorce from the natural world, which surrounds us whether we can perceive it or not. In the service of those few foods we've built our modern diet on — corn, wheat, beef, rice — we have carpeted our nation with non-native species; only corn has its origin in this hemisphere. And when those immigrants run wild over the landscape, they become destroyers and usurpers of our meadows, rivers, and forests.

They are a plague on an already stressed ecosystem. Wild fennel, so highly prized in Italy, is a scourge of the countryside where I live in Northern California. The dandelions in your yard are the same; they too hail from Europe. Wild hogs till our hillsides, mangling native grasses and wildflowers. Once-migratory Canada geese foul our parks and ponds. Strange fish empty our reefs and rivers of its former denizens, leaving a watery wasteland in their wake.

But these exotic invaders are all prized foods somewhere else. Carp in China and Germany. Iguanas in Mexico. Tilapia in Africa.

It is this last fish that gives hope to the notion that we can eat our way out of this mess, or at least consume to contain it. Tilapia is among the most popular fish eaten in the United States; it is one of the few "new" foods mainstream America has embraced in the past decades. Yet few know it has become an invader in our subtropical states.

We were not always so narrow-minded in our food choices, and not every place in the United States is so limited in its menu even today. Alligator, turtle, and frog are commonly eaten in Louisiana. Muskrat can be had at diners on the East Coast's Delmarva Peninsula. No one blinks at the idea of rattlesnake on a menu in Texas. And smoked eel has been a traditional part of Christmas among the Italian community of New York and New Jersey for more than a century.

It is not such a leap then, to consider eating something new. Is a Caribbean lionfish, with its poisonous spines, really any different from the highly sought-after Pacific rock cod, some of which can sport similarly poisonous spines? How different can iguana be from rattlesnake, or alligator? A nutria is just a giant muskrat, and both have meat that isn't much different from the high-priced hares that appear on fancy French menus.

And those are just the "hard" choices. Some of the invasives in this book are already mainstream fare for America's hunting community. More than one million waterfowlers take to the nation's marshes and grain fields each fall and winter in search of Canada geese. A similar number of big game hunters seek to fill their freezers with wild boar each year.

Because commercial hunting of Canada geese has been forbidden by the International Migratory Bird Treaty Act since 1918 — even though the geese discussed in this book no longer migrate — the prospect of finding shrink-wrapped Canada goose at your local Whole Foods is dim at best. But wild hogs are considered a pestilence on the land. There is no reason not to open a commercial market for them, and you can't get any more free-range than wild.

Cooked properly, all of these invasive animals can be fine fare. But there is another reason to put them on your menu: They are all here because of us. We have irrevocably altered the American landscape, and in the cases cited in this book, those alterations have deeply damaged the health of our waters, our meadows, and even our back yards. We created this mess. It is only fair that we do our bit to help clean it up.

— Hank Shaw

A former professional cook and newspaper reporter, Hank Shaw is author of Hunt, Gather, Cook: Finding the Forgotten Feast *and runs the award-winning wild foods blog Hunter Angler Gardener Cook. He hunts, forages, fishes, and cooks in northern California.*

Introduction

THE NATURE I SEE AROUND MY HOME in Virginia is not particularly natural. Sure, I can stand in a field, surrounded by plants, without a building in sight. Birds sing and insects buzz through the air. Upon close inspection, though, it becomes clear that most of these creatures don't actually belong here.

Dandelions, brought to America by European colonists who grew the plant in gardens as a vegetable, sprout everywhere. They're visited by European honeybees, which are (as their name indicates) also nonnative. Crabgrass, tree of paradise, the Japanese beetle, and the Asian lady beetle are everywhere, and they're all invaders. In the trees, imported starlings and sparrows congregate in vast flocks, denying nesting cavities to our native bluebirds and purple martins.

Beyond my own backyard, North America is besieged by bigger creatures that were introduced in folly. Across California and much of the South, feral swine root up large areas of ground, transforming the habitat and causing erosion. They eat native salamanders and the eggs of ground-nesting birds. Asian carp, some coming in at more than fifty pounds, eat up to forty percent of their body weight in plant matter every day. Long stretches of the Missouri River are now populated almost exclusively by invasive carp, and the native fish are pushed closer and closer to extinction.

Florida may be past all hope, with the Everglades riddled with some two hundred thousand reticulated pythons eating their way through what was once a delicately balanced ecosystem. In many parts of the state, iguanas up to six feet long devour every plant in sight. With no local predators adapted to eating them, they reproduce unchecked. Nile monitor lizards, often five feet long, hunt along suburban Florida canals, preying on household pets and whatever other small animals venture too close.

Each of these creatures individually is doing what its instinct tells it to do. In their sum, though, they are forcing many native plants and animals to the brink of extinction. In each of these cases, there have been efforts by state and federal wildlife agencies to remove the destructive invaders. Money is spent, good science is done, but government programs have been unable to keep up with the scale of the problem.

It's easy to shrug and say the problem is so big, the numbers of starlings and carp so great, that humans couldn't possibly get rid of them all. But consider that human beings have historically succeeded in eliminating animals in such numbers. Recklessly, we've driven many formerly plentiful species to extinction or to extirpation from a section of their range. The difference is motivation, not capability.

The passenger pigeon is an example of an animal people have killed and eaten into extinction. In 1800, the passenger pigeon was the most plentiful bird in the Americas and perhaps in the world. There were billions of them in North America alone. One hundred and fourteen years later, there was just one — one pigeon, named Martha, who died in her cage at the Cincinnati Zoo in 1914. What happened?

People happened. In their vast flocks, numbering in the millions, pigeons could be shot in great numbers by market hunters, who sold the meat to grocers. Passenger pigeon became the least expensive meat you could buy; it was the chicken of its day. In the absence of bag limits and meaningful hunting regulations, there was no check on the desire for personal gain that motivated the shooting.

What would have happened if nobody wanted to eat passenger pigeons? Certainly the species was in trouble anyway, because of habitat loss, but if people hadn't developed a taste for the bird, there might still be large flocks of them today.

CAN THIS HUMAN ABILITY TO HARVEST WILD FOOD in dangerously efficient ways be harnessed for a good ecological cause? I believe it can. If invasive species such as starlings and Asian carp were rediscovered by Americans as desirable food sources, we would clear our sky and water of them, just as surely as we've wiped out so many native plants and animals.

Really, what we choose to eat is often a matter of perspective and tradition rather than an informed judgment based on what something tastes like. Most of these problem species have either previously been considered to be good eating by humans or still are by people in other parts of the world. Asian carp is a beloved food in China. The Spanish make starlings into a prized pâté. Iguanas have been eaten as a staple protein in most of their native range — from Mexico to Brazil — for thousands of years.

Fortunately, there is a precedent for Americans doing a complete about-face on the suitability of odd-looking creatures for food. During colonial times, lobsters were considered edible only by the most desperate segments of the population. Household servants would include provisions in their contracts stating that they could not be fed lobster more than four times a week. Today, lobster sells for around ten dollars a pound at the grocery store — more than most cuts of beef. What transformed lobster from peasant food into a delicacy was simply a change in perspective.

In North America, with hundreds of species of native plants, birds, insects, and animals threatened by alien species, it's time we started changing our perspective. By hunting and eating invasive animals, we can help restore habitat for native species, as well as reduce our dependence on factory-farmed meat and eat more locally, thus decreasing the costs associated with transportation (odds are, there are edible invasives to be found close to your own home). If you're going to eat meat, you might as well do it in a way that's ecologically helpful. In some cases, I've found that invasive species could be harvested on a commercial scale and sold. In other cases, only a grassroots effort by dedicated locavores will be practical.

It's quite an emotional leap to make, especially for those of us who didn't grow up hunting and fishing, but it's one that can be made, with practice and experience. As a professional hunting instructor who teaches adult beginners and grew up in a vegetarian household, I have a lot of sympathy for people who are slowly warming up to the idea of killing for food. Understand, though, that the skills and tools I describe throughout this book can be acquired, and it's possible to overcome the normal reluctance to, for example, gut and scale a fish.

Part of what makes this leap possible is the realization that you're playing a part in helping to fix an ecological disaster in progress. If you can do this, you'll feel better about your place in the world. Your food will have a deeper meaning than the price tag and calorie count, and you'll value the time you spent outdoors in pursuit of it. Making the leap changed my life, and it could change yours, too.

WHILE WRITING THIS BOOK, I spent about sixteen months traveling around the United States and the Caribbean, hunting and fishing for invasive species. The process didn't happen quite the way that I'd expected it would, however. Not every species turned out to be the problem that it had been made out to be; at the same time, I ran into other invasive species I'd had no idea were even out there.

In the beginning, I thought I was hitting the road simply to find and eat invasive wildlife. It usually turned out that the bigger issues were with human beings. Human activity has caused the introduction of many invasive species that threaten the survival of native wildlife. Every invasive species is native somewhere, and in most cases that is the place where we should have left it.

Black Spiny-Tailed Iguanas

“I wish I never had to kill another living thing,” George remarked, a serious look on his broad, suntanned face. “There’s nothing good about having to do any of this. But I know that for every ctenosaur I shoot, I’m saving hundreds of other native animals. The only thing worse than having to kill sixteen thousand iguanas would be watching all of these other animals go extinct.”

To paraphrase Noël Coward, the only creatures foolish enough to venture out in the midday sun in the tropics are mad dogs and Englishmen. Not fitting into either of these categories, I nevertheless found myself in the Florida sun at noon, on Gasparilla Island, improbably riding shotgun in a golf cart while hiding a pellet rifle under my backpack as we drove past the vacation home of George W. Bush's brother Marvin. There was, in fact, an Englishman (a journalist named Jeff Latham) sitting in the backseat, but no mad dogs were in sight. Our prey was the black spiny-tailed iguana.

The golf cart was piloted by George Cera, professional hunter and trapper of nuisance animals. George likes to refer to the spiny-tail as a "ctenosaur" (TEEN-a-sore), which makes sense for two reasons. First, it's close to the animal's Latin name — *Ctenosaura similis.* Second, the word *ctenosaur* makes it sound like we're talking about a dinosaur. Once you've seen a ctenosaur up close, you'll find the comparison to be apt. Its scaly head, sharp teeth, and short crest along the top of its back make it look like something from the Jurassic period.

The spiny-tailed iguana is a distant relative of the better-known green iguana, which is frequently kept as a pet. Their silhouettes are somewhat similar in profile, but the black-and-gray coloring of the adult spiny-tailed iguana immediately sets it apart. The two are further differentiated by their eating habits. The green is almost exclusively an herbivore; the spiny-tail is an omnivore. Although it's happy to eat leaves, buds, and fruit, it will pounce on almost anything that moves and is small enough to swallow. Because the male tops out at almost five feet long , quite a lot of things are small enough for it to ingest.

The spiny-tail is well equipped to have its way with other creatures. Its weaponry consists chiefly of a row of very sharp front teeth, which are angled steeply back into the mouth to hold on to whatever it can grab. If the teeth haven't convinced an opponent to either run away or get into the ctenosaur's belly, the four sets of pointed black talons should be persuasive. If the thing isn't worth trying to eat, the sharp scutes — horny scales — along the tail turn it into a formidable whip that the lizard can and will use in combat. Those scutes are sharp enough that they can draw blood even when the lizard is dead. If the fight doesn't seem to be going the spiny-tail's way, it can instantly disconnect its own tail and leave the wriggling, disembodied member as a distraction while it makes its escape.

The spiny-tail also uses its weaponry to claim its living space. It likes to sleep and hide in holes, and will dig one for itself if it must, but it prefers one that some other animal has already dug, and then "makes arrangements" for its use. That often consists of biting the hell out of its former owner. If possible, the invader will eat the occupant and its offspring.

The spiny-tailed iguanas on Gasparilla Island are descended from a handful that were deliberately released by an exotic-pet owner who was no longer willing to take care of them. A very apologetic gentleman has admitted to being the culprit about thirty years ago. At the time, he'd had no idea what he was unleashing on the island. This is a confession that has, unfortunately, been repeated with many different species by pet owners in Florida. An animal may become too large or aggressive to care for, or perhaps the owner is moving to a place that prohibits pets. Unwilling to euthanize what was a pet, the owner releases it in a patch of woods and hopes for the best.

If this were to happen in New Jersey, say, that lizard or snake or other exotic animal would probably have an exciting summer before falling asleep on a cold day in October or November and never waking up. In a subtropical environment like Florida's, an exotic pet from Africa or South America might very well live to reproduce.

Initially, the iguanas were a novel delight to watch creeping around gardens, and they became a constant presence on every block of Boca Grande (the town in which we were hunting). In typical human fashion, most of the town's residents decided this was a problem only when the iguanas actually began to *devour* their gardens. By the time I came to Gasparilla Island, many plants hadn't flowered in years; the spiny-tails can easily climb even the tallest plants and eat the flower buds before they open. This problem prompted the town officials of Boca Grande to hire George. What he found when he started hunting the iguanas was something far more sinister than damage to ornamental plants.

George, Jeff, and I drove a few blocks farther, occasionally slowing down as we passed empty vacation homes where George had permission to hunt iguanas. Even though it was legal to carry a pellet rifle and shoot iguanas, we tried to keep the gun out of sight: You never know when some tourist will overreact, call the police, and create a messy situation that wastes everyone's time. We paused for a few minutes in front of a large yard to watch a pair of big males sunning themselves. George put a hand on his pellet rifle but didn't shoulder it. Suddenly, one of the lizards leapt into the air at a shocking speed and grabbed what looked to be a small brown anole (a smaller species of lizard) off the side of a stump. That's another thing about spiny-tailed iguanas: They hold the record as the fastest lizards on the planet.

The electric cart squeaked to a stop in front of a broad empty lot, and Jeff and I hopped out. Jeff happened to be writing a story about George at the same time I'd arrived to go hunting with him. I suppose Jeff might have expected to spend a few days doing interviews and taking a few pictures, but the morning he walked through George's front door, we hustled him out into the cart to come hunting with us.

We approached a half-moon-shaped hole in the ground, and I noted the spiderwebs across the top of the hole, which, I surmised aloud, indicated that nothing large could be living there at the moment. As we looked around for the probable occupant of the hole, Jeff spotted a surprisingly large gopher tortoise staring at us from the dappled sunlight under a tree. The tortoise looked at each of us in turn, seemingly unafraid and already bored with us. (I suppose if you've been facing down big, black-and-gray lizards with teeth like those of a prehistoric crocodile for the last ten years, you're not likely to be easily scared off.) After a minute, it ambled into the hole I'd insisted was uninhabited.

In Florida, the native gopher tortoise is a keystone species — that is, a plant or animal that many other species depend on for survival. It happens to be a keystone for some three hundred other species. It digs holes up to forty feet long, in locations that don't tend to cause erosion or environmental damage but that do provide homes for many other animals. There are also fruits, such as the gopher apple and the saw palmetto, that the gopher tortoise helps to reproduce. It spreads the seeds in its droppings, thus aiding propagation. The gopher tortoise tends to excrete seeds intact and ready to germinate more often than do many of the other animals that eat the same fruit.

We saw many gopher tortoises during the three days I spent in Boca Grande, but none of them had a shell smaller than about seven or eight inches long. It wasn't difficult to figure out why: The iguanas were eating all of the eggs and hatchlings before they could grow large enough to be safe from most predation. It wouldn't be a stretch to assume that if this keeps up, the species will disappear from the island.

Other species are in danger as well. George told me he once witnessed a nest of baby scrub jays (an endangered species) being cleaned out by an iguana. By the time he returned to the nest with a pellet rifle, it was too late. It isn't known how many species of bird are at risk to spiny-tail predation; the research simply hasn't been done. Given that this lizard is equally comfortable in treetops and in underground tunnels, a wide variety of bird species could be in grave danger of extinction.

On our second day of cruising the streets and culs-de-sac of Boca Grande, it was my turn to shoot. In Florida, no special license is required to hunt animals that are designated as nuisance species, and the air rifles we were using are exempt from the prohibitions on discharging a firearm in town. At first, it seemed absurd to refer to cruising around in a golf cart as hunting. But after having shot iguanas with George, I can honestly say that this qualified. There's a knack to it. Understanding what type of environmental "structure" (types of plants and proximity to hiding places, for example) the lizards prefer is most of the challenge.

Positively identifying one is a challenge; after a while, *everything* started to look like an iguana: shadows, sticks, even figments of my imagination. George's trick is to stop looking for an iguana. Instead, he looks for something that doesn't belong: a shape or a shadow that doesn't quite fit with patterns in the landscape. Sometimes that shape is a chunk of palm-tree bark on the ground; at other times it's the broken end of a branch protruding from one of the banyan trees that have turned several streets on the island into haunting, leafy caves. And every now and then, it just might be a big invasive lizard.

These days, it's less likely that the out-of-place shadow will prove to be a spiny-tail. That's because George has single-handedly killed more than sixteen thousand of the lizards on Gasparilla. Some lucky town employee was assigned to count the fruits of George's bounty from a ripe-smelling trash can at the end of every day. By the time I arrived, the once-booming population had been reduced to a relatively few adults and a great many of the diminutive green juveniles: enough to bring back the problem in a big way in just a few years, if the hunting pressure lets up.

We cruised around looking for my first kill. It was early in the day and the action was slow. Iguanas don't seem to be out and about reliably until between noon and 1 p.m. A pickup truck passed us heading the other way and George glared at it.

"USDA guys," George said, furrowing the brow of his shaved head. "Those guys have no frickin' clue what they're doing. Nothing but a pain in my ass. Guess how many lizards they take, on average, each day they're out there."

He shifted his bulk in the seat to stare at them.

"Seven." He answered his own question, disgusted.

"And how many were you taking right before the town put them in charge?" I asked.

"Around thirty."

I couldn't imagine what the U.S. Department of Agriculture would be doing in a small town on an island fueled by the businesses of tourism and tarpon fishing, with nary a farm or ranch in sight.

What happened was this: After George had just about pounded the spiny-tails into submission, the USDA decided it wanted in on the action. During the last few decades, the agency has managed to expand the scope of its funding and efforts against invasive species beyond farms and into suburban neighborhoods, state parks, and pretty much anywhere else it can find them. In theory, this should be a good thing. In the case of Gasparilla Island, what it meant was that the guy who had proved that he was able to dramatically reduce the population was replaced by agents of a much less efficient government bureaucracy.

George Cera had lost the town's iguana-control contract after the USDA muscled in and convinced the local government to end the open-bidding process. Yet here he was, still cruising around, removing iguanas from properties whose owners had granted him permission. He had technically become a volunteer — he wasn't getting paid a dime for this. He believed it was the right thing to do.

We saw the USDA guys many times during my visit. They drove around in their pickup truck as fast as the speed limit would allow. George cruised slowly in his golf cart, watching every detail and pulling the maneuverable cart along paths too small for a conventional vehicle. With no windshield or doors to impede a shot, he could quickly take out a spiny-tail that would have spooked had he tried to get out of the cart. It was easy to understand some of the reasons that George had been so successful during his tenure as the town lizard catcher. Watching the routine of the USDA team, I understood why there were now so many juvenile iguanas darting across sidewalks and pouncing on anoles.

One of those plentiful and charismatic green juveniles soon offered itself as my first target. It was sunning itself on a brick sidewalk, and cocked its head and bobbed up and down in challenge to my presence. At a scant fifteen yards away, a shot like that would be a cinch with a .22 on a squirrel or other small mammal. The only thing was that I wasn't using a .22 and my prey wasn't a mammal. I was forced to hunt with an air rifle that shoots .17-caliber pellets and I had to put one of those pellets directly into the lizard's brain or upper spine.

One of the funny things about reptiles is that they take a little longer than mammals do to acknowledge the fact that they're dead.

A snake once made a nuisance of itself in my house. After killing, gutting, and skinning it, I put the meat directly on the charcoal grill (dipped in barbecue sauce, it was excellent). While the snake was cooking, I observed that its heart continued to beat on the ground for a full hour after being removed. Many reptiles have this shocking resilience. A bullet through the lungs that would take down most other animals may inspire an iguana to run a hundred yards into a mangrove swamp and never be recovered.

This is a problem for two reasons. First, every hunter has an obligation to ensure the least amount of suffering for the prey. Second, my intent is to cook and eat the animals I hunt, and that doesn't work if I can't find them after I shoot them.

I figured the only way to be absolutely certain the iguana wouldn't run off after it was hit would be to destroy the central nervous system at once, with a shot either to the brain or to the upper spine. In this case, the animal might still be moving its limbs reflexively, but not in any deliberate way, and certainly the motion wouldn't take it any farther afield.

I'd seen George take many shots like this off-hand (that is, without any solid object or special position to steady the rifle), but I didn't think I could match his shooting skills. I got down on one knee, sighted on the back of the iguana's head, and squeezed the trigger.

The small green lizard thrashed around briefly, then lay still. I picked it up and smacked its head against the sidewalk, just in case. This proved unnecessary, as I had sent the pellet straight through the iguana's head.

I felt a little sad holding the lifeless five-inch body. It was kind of cute, and I understood why people took them home from pet stores. Nobody would look at this creature and imagine that it would eventually turn into a miniature dinosaur with virtual blades on its tail, devouring nestlings and baby gopher tortoises.

That day, I took other, larger iguanas as well. I never failed to hit my target in the head, although my ability to visualize the position of the brain in three dimensions from any angle could not equal George's.

In one case my lizard, a barely mature male of about fourteen inches, started to bolt from a shot that was a bit off to one side and George anchored it for me with a shot from his rifle. The creature still managed to scuttle into the hollow center of an old railroad tie during the second or two before it expired. We had hell's own fun turning the eight-foot-long hunk of wood on end and chopping out the dead iguana with the hatchet that I carry around for just this sort of thing.

We could usually stalk to within twenty yards of a spiny-tail before it bolted. The critters spooked much less easily in the early days of George's work. Also, hunting iguanas in a densely built-up area like Boca Grande meant that it was often necessary to pass up an easy shot because there was a house nearby. We'd either move on and look for another one or get into position for a safer angle that involved a longer range. Anything over fifty yards is probably asking for trouble on a larger iguana, though. The light .17-caliber pellet loses velocity over distance and might not make a clean kill, even when perfectly aimed.

Hunting iguanas requires more ability as a marksman than most other types of hunting I've participated in. For example, to hunt deer, you must be able to place your shot into a circle of about seven inches in diameter. That is roughly the size of the lungs when seen from broadside. Such a shot will reliably kill the deer, and though it may run a few dozen yards before dropping, it's not usually hard to find. It's not difficult for a novice hunter to learn to place five consecutive shots into a seven-inch-diameter circle and, as a professional hunting instructor, I've rarely encountered anyone who couldn't do this out to at least fifty yards after an hour of practice.

The target area of an iguana, on the other hand, is much smaller. Even a large spiny-tail has a brain of only about the size of a large marble. It takes a great deal of practice to learn how to shoot that accurately under field conditions. Fortunately, this practice is inexpensive either with a conventional .22 rifle or with the lead pellets used by an air rifle.

Boca Grande was almost deserted during my visit. In the off-season, the island is left to a handful of hardy full-time residents who aren't in a position to be fussy about the brand of their beer when it costs eighteen bucks for a twelve-pack of the cheap stuff. Island prices hurt, and the four-dollar bridge toll tends to discourage unnecessary trips. You don't do anything in a hurry in mid-September off the Gulf Coast of Florida, unless it's on fire or on sale. In-season, the place fills up with the people who own or rent the multimillion-dollar houses that George hunts around. I guess it's not so bad if you're the guy selling the eighteen-dollar beer.

Although there weren't a lot of people around, there was plenty of wildlife. There were large and exotic wading birds of all descriptions: elegant tricolored ibises, snowy egrets, and the same great blue herons that I knew from back home in Virginia. I watched an endangered scrub jay fly across the road between patches of mangroves. Those birds had almost been extirpated from the island when the spiny-tails were at their worst.

George's girlfriend, Cindy, managed to set us up with one of the only two restaurants still open in Boca Grande during this final stretch of the off-season: South Beach Restaurant, a watering hole that draws maintenance workers, property managers, and the odd bunch of tourists. Jeff and I bellied up to the bar and ordered pints of cold, bitter beer.

The chef, Greg Beano — a round, pleasant middle-aged man with a perpetually serene look on his face — hurried out of the kitchen to introduce himself, and proposed that we turn the iguanas into a plate of tacos. We carried our beers, bags, and a cooler full of almost frozen spiny-tailed iguanas into the hot, loud kitchen and got to work. I took a lizard and set it on a white plastic cutting board. It didn't look like food so much as a prop from one of the *Gremlins* movies.

Most of the meat on an iguana is in the limbs and tail. There's some over the ribs, but unless you're working with exceptionally large lizards, it's not likely to be enough to bother chasing for food.

I drew my hunting knife from its sheath and began slicing off the limbs. The bones proved stiffer and tougher than I had expected. For the second time that day, I reached for the hatchet on my belt. I gave the thick hind limb a mighty chop, and it came right off.

"Stay out of the digestive system," cautioned George. "It will stink all to hell if you go in there. Seriously, don't even think about gutting it."

As I chopped off the tail, I did indeed go too high up the body, and the back of the digestive system opened. George was right. The funk was at least as bad as gutting a turkey (which, trust me, can make you think about switching to tofu for Thanksgiving). I carried what was left of the iguana out the back door and chucked it into a trash can.

After we'd butchered all our lizards, we had a pile of scaly, dismembered limbs bearing menacing black claws, mixed with sharply armored tails. This still didn't look like food. Chef Greg parboiled the limbs and then dunked them immediately into cold water to loosen up the hide. Peeling the skin off the flesh took some time but was easier than, say, picking crabmeat.

With the hide off, we began pulling the meat from the bones and shredding it by hand. We avoided the bright yellow fat, as it has an unpleasant taste and smell. This fat is isolated into tiny pockets around the surface rather than marbled throughout the meat, so it wasn't difficult to keep it out of our pile of the good stuff.

Pulled from the bone and filling a medium-size bowl, the iguana meat finally looked like food.

Greg whipped up a marinade of lime, cilantro, tequila, and a few spices. He browned the meat in a pan and served the tacos in soft shells with a nice salsa verde. Now it *smelled* like food.

We sat at a table on the patio with another round of beers, and Greg carried the platter of tacos out to us. With only the slightest hesitation, we each took our first bite. It was pretty good. It was *very* good. George aptly described it as tasting like chicken with the texture of crab.

Later that night, we sat on plastic lawn chairs in George's shell-covered driveway as the sun sank over the ocean. I propped up my feet on a cooler full of iguanas and cracked open a beer.

"I wish I never had to kill another living thing," George remarked, a serious look on his broad, suntanned face. "There's nothing good about having to do any of this. But I know that for every ctenosaur I shoot, I'm saving hundreds of other native animals. The only thing worse than having to kill sixteen thousand iguanas would be watching all of these other animals go extinct."

I imagined what the trash cans full of dead, bloody iguanas must have looked and smelled like when George began the task of cleaning up the island. It doesn't seem likely that a man would create such a mess day after day, for not much more than a living wage, without some greater sense of purpose.

Green
Iguanas

With a crash course in lizard hunting under my belt, I said goodbye to my new friends in Boca Grande. My father-in-law, Bob, and I packed the pop-up camper and started the long drive from Gasparilla Island down to the Florida Keys.

Rather than deal with the monotony of Alligator Alley, the parkway that cuts across the Everglades from one side of Florida to the other, we took a much smaller road farther south. Route 40 seemed weird and out of the way, which is usually what I'm looking for.

We passed through miles of swampland bordered by tall palm trees, short scrubby pines, and pools of standing water filled with a vast variety of wading birds. Here and there, a billboard or hand-lettered sign advertised airboat tours and guaranteed alligator sightings. Occasionally, we could see buildings through the trees. The first ones we saw were fairly conventional boxes with gabled or flat roofs, but later we started to see roofs that appeared to be made of thatched palm leaves. These were the homes of Seminole Indians, still living on their traditional lands. In the uncompromising swamps of southern Florida, the U.S. Army never managed to push out the last of these people, or round them up the way they did across most of the rest of the continent. Between the saw grass, the snakes, the heat, and the alligators, it takes a special kind of desperation and cunning to stick around.

The Seminole roofs and gator tours gradually gave way to a long stretch of fruit farms and palm-tree nurseries. Route 40 eventually spilled us out into the urban sprawl of Dade County. We met up with Route A1A, of Jimmy Buffett fame, which took us straight down to the Keys. The scenery segued into cheap sandal shops, boat dealers, and chintzy seafood restaurants built to look like boats.

On Big Pine Key, I stood in the office at an RV park. I handed my credit card to the woman behind the counter and subtly tried to get tips about where to hunt.

"So you have a lot of wildlife right around here, huh?"

"Oh, we've got the Keys deer everywhere." She handed me a slip of paper to sign.

"What about green iguanas?" I asked. "You see any of those?"

"All the time. I get about a dozen real big ones in my backyard every day. They hang out by the pool and eat the grass. Five feet long. I love watching them out there."

I smiled and handed her back the signed credit-card receipt. This didn't seem like the best moment to suggest that I go to her place and shoot a bunch of enormous lizards.

THE WOMAN'S REACTION represents one of the biggest impediments to managing many invasive species. Unless an animal is destroying the landscaping or eating the cat, people tend to enjoy seeing an exotic species in the backyard. Green iguanas are almost exclusively herbivorous and will not bite unless directly provoked. They're charismatic-looking creatures, especially as juveniles. Sometimes they appear to be smiling slightly, with an almost smug look about them, as though they know something you don't. Millions of people keep green iguanas as pets. It isn't surprising, then, that many Floridians enjoy observing them in the wild.

The native range for green iguanas is throughout Central and South America, along with a few Caribbean islands. The climate of southern Florida is similar enough to that of these places that it's no surprise that iguanas have thrived there as well. Local legend claims that green iguanas first came to the Keys as stowaways on ships carrying fruit from South America.

Even in my hometown of Charlottesville, Virginia, there are stories about exotic stowaways being released into the old pink warehouse by the railroad tracks. In the 1990s, my brother lived in a cavernous apartment carved out of the top level, and the lore among the residents was that back in the 1950s they would unload bananas from the trains and store them in the warehouse. They said you had to watch out back then, because the warehouse was crawling with tarantulas, small pythons, and other creatures that had ridden on the bananas all the way from South America. If they escaped from the warehouse, they'd die when autumn arrived and the temperature dropped.

The green iguanas on the mainland were first noticed in Miami-Dade County in the 1960s. Although no one knows for sure how they arrived, many people speculate that they were either stowaways in a shipment of fruit or former pets that were released into the wild. As is often the case with an invasive species, the vector of introduction is difficult to pinpoint.

Part of the problem with green iguanas in the Keys is that they have a strong preference for eating the nicker nut, a plant that also happens to be the primary food source of the endangered Miami blue butterfly. The only remaining population of these pretty butterflies is on Bahia Honda Key, right next to Big Pine. Take away too many of the nicker nuts, and the Miami blue butterfly will become extinct. As of today, it's been a few years since anyone has seen one.

At the RV park, my father-in-law and I set up the camper and sat at a picnic table beside it. A strong wind was coming straight off the water, which was only about thirty yards away. Somewhere out in the Caribbean, a hurricane was churning up the surf. We looked around at the omnipresent campground maintenance workers and contemplated the difficulty of the task at hand. On Gasparilla Island, I'd had the benefit of a local hunter to work with. He and I had land access and local knowledge. Down on Big Pine Key, Bob and I didn't have any of that, but we did have a bunch of locals who thought our prey was cute.

Hunting green iguanas and most other invasive species in the Keys is legal, as long as you mind exactly where you do it. Much of Big Pine is a federal refuge for a diminutive subspecies of white-tail deer known as the Key deer. Walking around on refuge land with an air rifle is likely to get you picked up by a Fish and Wildlife officer for attempting to poach deer.

Most of the land that isn't part of the refuge consists of residential neighborhoods, and hunting invasive species with an air rifle is perfectly legal there. Still, I'd have to expect witnesses to pitch a fit and call 911. Sure, I'd be on the right side of the law, as long as I wasn't trespassing on private property, but this wasn't a situation I wanted to find myself in.

For about two days we scouted. It quickly became clear that there were green iguanas everywhere; it was equally clear that I was going to have a rough time closing the deal with any of them. Most of the iguanas I was seeing were either on private property I had no access to or in spots where it would be awkward to shoot.

After spending some time cruising for green iguanas, we identified certain environments that looked like potential iguana habitat: open, grassy areas with a few shrubs, bordering thick mangroves or similar cover near water. Agile climbers as well as swimmers, green iguanas seem to prefer being close to water or thick cover or both, in order to have something to escape into. We weren't going to be able to get any green iguanas by cruising slowly down the streets, the way I had when I was hunting for black spiny-tails with

George Cera on Gasparilla Island; I would have to find a promising area and get dropped off to go in on foot, commando-style.

Back at camp, I checked off a list of supplies to bring in with me on my mission. Air rifle, check. Lead pellets, check. Binoculars, belt hatchet, water, camouflage, hunting knife, video camera, plastic bags to hold the meat, first-aid kit, and a cell phone to call for a ride upon completion of the mission: all check.

Bob drove me down a long access road that went off into the bush and eventually came to a dead end. There were no federal refuge signs and nothing that said NO TRESPASSING. He came to a stop near a place that looked as if it might be harboring iguanas, and I got out. He drove off, back toward civilization, and I melted into the mangroves as quickly as I could.

It had seemed like a good idea to wear a pair of soft-soled water shoes instead of the combat boots that I usually favor while hunting; with the swampy terrain, I figured I might end up in the water. A few dozen spike-covered seedpods poking into my bleeding soles were an excellent argument against that decision. There was nothing for it: I gingerly pulled them out, and almost as quickly acquired more.

I came upon an abandoned, boarded-up building in a clearing with grass up to my knees. This looked like green iguana territory for certain. I walked around the building and, sure enough, there was as big an iguana as I'd ever seen, lying on top of a crumbling stone wall.

Right away I backed up and crept to the corner of the building. I dropped to one knee and steadied the air rifle for a shot of about thirty yards. Remembering what I had learned from George while hunting the spiny-tails, I lined up for a brain shot.

I hoped the brain of a green iguana would be in about the same part of the head as on its carnivorous relatives.

As the shot hit, the front of the iguana dropped to the other side of the wall while the back end remained visible. I jogged over to it and awkwardly attempted to reload the air rifle on my way.

The back legs still gripped the stone, but the great lizard didn't react to my presence. It seemed as dead as a reptile can get in that short amount of time, which is admittedly not very dead. Just in case, I put another shot into the head.

It was a male, somewhere north of four feet long. There was nothing green about this green iguana. He had a magnificent reddish dewlap, and the rest of him was gray with a mottling of other colors, ending with a black-and-white-checkered tail.

Lacking ice or refrigeration in the Florida heat, I decided to butcher the iguana immediately. This lizard was much bigger than the ones we had taken on Gasparilla Island, so rather than try to chop through its heavy bones, it made sense to take it apart the same way I'd butcher a whitetail deer.

Figuring that the basic relationships between the major bones would be similar to those of deer, I made the first incisions on all four limbs from the abdominal side and then brought the cut up. This is much easier than trying to do it from the top down.

The tail proved a little trickier. It was much bigger than that of the spiny-tailed iguanas we'd worked with on Gasparilla Island. I chopped at the thick, heavy tail a few ways, then, suddenly, it dropped off on its own, disconnecting right where I'd wanted it to. The disembodied tail twitched and thrashed for a moment and then lay still. I looked at the open cut and saw a smooth, W-shaped mass of muscle.

I assumed that this reaction was the result of two things: the slow death process a lizard goes through (which hadn't at that point reached the tail) and that, like many other species of lizard, the green iguana is capable of dropping off its tail when attacked. The predator is distracted by the thrashing tail and can even eat it as a consolation prize, and the lizard escapes to live another day and eventually grow another tail. Sometimes more than one tail grows from the stump.

As a child reading books about natural history, I had often wondered whether the tail dropping was voluntary. Now, seeing that big green iguana release its tail when its brain was defunct and the remains were half-butchered suggested a reflex that doesn't rely on a functioning central nervous system. I was intrigued.

I put the limbs and tail into a plastic bag and stuffed it into my backpack. I threw the head and torso into the brush to feed the scavengers, although later I regretted not saving the entire hide to preserve as a curiosity.

I hunted a little longer before deciding to quit while I was ahead, and called Bob to come and get me. We were going to try our hand at cooking up the iguana. I had all of the ingredients to make a pasta sauce, so I figured we'd make some iguana pasta for dinner that evening.

Our cooking venue — the kitchenette of the pop-up camper — was quite a bit more cramped than the kitchen on Gasparilla Island where Greg Beano was showing us how to make iguana tacos. It also had limited facilities: a three-burner gas range and only the most basic utensils.

The hide of a large green iguana is thick and strong; it would be great material for making belts, books, knife sheaths, perhaps even for backing a traditional wooden bow. Unfortunately, the easiest way to skin a lizard to get at the meat — by parboiling it — pretty much ruins the hide, so I decided to try a different method. With a pocketknife, I skinned each limb by making a short incision from the cut end. Then I stuck the gut hook of my hunting knife into that incision and pulled it down to the reptile's foot. This gave me access to the length of the inside, and I had two sides of hide to pull apart. This worked all right on the limbs, but the tail was a real piece of work; that hide was very tightly attached to the flesh and just wouldn't come off. I had to continually work the blade along every bit of hide.

Because the meat is all in the tail and legs, gutting is unnecessary. This means that an iguana is actually easier to butcher than poultry is. Iguana is much easier to process than fish is, too; there are far fewer bones. I carved the raw flesh from the bones with a small knife, minced it on a cutting board (for lack of a meat grinder in my bare-bones kitchen), and sautéed it in olive oil with a little garlic. I whipped up a basic American-style ragout sauce using the iguana meat as a substitute for the more common beef or pork.

Like its spiny-tailed cousin, green iguana turns out to taste pretty much like chicken. Late that night, Bob and I finished our plates of spaghetti and iguana sauce and walked the dozen or so yards to the ocean with our fishing rods and some beer. The wind blew in from a tropical storm that was brewing a few hundred miles out. I cast my line into the moonlit water and wondered what would happen if even a fraction of the recreational fishermen in Florida took up iguana hunting as a pastime.

It's not an easy state in which to hunt: The same swampy tangle of vegetation that hid those last Seminoles won't give up invasive green iguanas any more readily. With a few more hunters, though, we might be able to at least hold them at bay, to provide a few places for plants like the nicker nut to grow and for species like the Miami blue butterfly to continue to exist. If Floridians could learn to eat the iguanas in their own backyards, it would make a very real difference.

Pigs
and Armadillos

HUMAN BEINGS HAVE LEFT A TRAIL of swine around the world. European explorers and colonists took pigs with them pretty much everywhere they went. Being particularly clever animals, pigs have the habit of escaping from captivity. As highly adaptable omnivores, they can survive and reproduce just about anywhere, making them one of the most widespread invasive species in the world.

Their release was often deliberate, on islands in particular. When Captain James Cook set out on his first voyage of exploration, he brought a large supply of pigs and goats to release on suitable islands, in order to provide a source of food for future stops by naval vessels. To trace his route around the world is to follow a series of ecological tragedies that continue to unfold as the descendants of Cook's livestock eat their way through native habitats.

When I got it into my head to hunt pigs, I started on Back Bay, which amounts to a barrier island connected to the mainland of Virginia by a narrow spit of land. The pigs of Back Bay are the descendants of escaped domestic swine. Although no one knows how long the pigs have been on the island, they're thought to have escaped about a hundred years ago.

With Bob, my father-in-law, again along for the ride, I drove to a campground a few miles from the Back Bay Wildlife Refuge. We took a cabin for the night or, rather, for a very small fraction thereof. There are a lot of rules about hunting Back Bay, and one of them is that everyone needs to be at the gate to sign in by four in the morning.

More rules: Shotguns only. No rifles, no muzzleloaders, no pistols, no bait. No spotlighting. No hunting outside of your assigned zone, on pain of arrest. The borders between zones won't be visible, so you'll just have to avoid moving around too much. No scouting, except in designated areas on special days.

No gutting or quartering your pigs, either. The refuge staff wants to examine the stomach contents and take samples. If you happen to shoot a three-hundred-pound animal two miles from the nearest road or trail, lots of luck getting it out of there. If a hunter from a neighboring zone helps you carry out your pig, he is now outside his zone and subject to arrest. State law requires that you carry your hunting license at all times while hunting, but the federal employees who manage this wildlife preserve require that all licenses be held at the desk while hunters are hunting, meaning that you're damned either way if someone in a uniform decides he doesn't like you. There's more: No walking on the beach. No shooting from any vehicle or boat.

The rules for hunting Back Bay probably give visiting hours at Folsom Prison a run for their money.

Bob and I found ourselves in a large, garagelike building waiting to check in before dawn. A few dozen hunters milled around in mismatched camouflage and blaze orange. They were all men, of various ages. Some stood in line in front of a row of folding tables, hunting licenses and signed papers in their hands. Others clustered in front of boards that showed how many pigs and deer had been taken from each zone on different days.

A parade of bureaucratic messes erupted between would-be hunters and the wildlife reserve employees. Hunters in their mid-sixties who had previously been told by game wardens that they were legally exempt from the requirement to present a hunter's education certificate were turned away. Tempers flared. The Fish and Wildlife officer, a frustrated-looking man in his late thirties, tried to keep order. It quickly became clear that he didn't know anything about Virginia's hunting regulations. In fact, he even declared that I would not be permitted to carry a weapon into the field, on account of missing paperwork. Bob and I briefly considered heading home but decided that Bob could carry his shotgun and I'd come along, unarmed, to help out.

The tension in the room between the hunters and the staff grew palpable as more hunters were given information that contradicted what they had been told before arriving. The Fish and Wildlife officer promised to check with a representative from the state wildlife agency about hunting regulations, and then reported back that nothing was going to change. I became curious as to who this state representative was. . . .

Finally, they hustled us all into open-sided shuttle vehicles that resembled the parking trams at Disney World. We were driven in total darkness and dropped off at spots that may or may not have been within our proper zones.

Bob and I stood in the middle of a gravel road as the red lights on the back of our vehicle disappeared into the distance. The ground was sodden from a recent heavy rain. We knew the dunes we needed to hunt were somewhere off to our left and that we had to get out to them before the sun came up. Pigs tend to go nocturnal when they've been hunted, and because hunting at night was forbidden, we needed to be in position for the first thirty minutes or so of daylight before the pigs were gone for the day. If you've got to hunt a nocturnal creature during the daytime, your best bet is to catch up with it at either the beginning or the end of its shift.

Getting to the dunes seemed essential. There, we'd be able to set up on a ridge or on the side of a dune with a view commanding a wide, open area. Everywhere else, there was too much vegetation and thus no visibility.

Our trouble was figuring out exactly how to get to where we wanted to be. In this restricted-access area, there were few hiking trails to follow. Nor had we been permitted to scout our zone in daylight before our arrival. The only thing we could do was to start walking straight for our destination and deal with whatever was in our way as best we could.

Lots of things tend to get in your way in the coastal swamps of Virginia. We made an initial effort to hop from hummock to hummock of grass in the flooded meadows near the road. But soon the water was deep enough that we went in up to our knees.

Bob began cursing up a storm, and I begged him to quiet down. We needed to be at least a little stealthy on our approach. His low-top hiking boots flooded much more quickly than did my water-resistant army boots. At least it was cold enough that we didn't need to worry about snakes. Not much, anyway. In addition to pigs, Back Bay is notable for representing the northernmost point of the range of the cottonmouth (also known as the water moccasin). We just hoped it would be too cold for any to be active.

Things turned ugly once we got into the bush. A wicked maze of thorns and low-branched bushes stood in our way, intermingled with fallen trees from past storms. I pulled out a pair of garden pruners from my pack and began clipping my way through the scrub. It was rough, but I knew it was unlikely that any thorns would kill me. In fact, I must confess to taking a certain bizarre pleasure in wading through the worst sorts of swamps and briars when circumstances call for it. There's a kind of freedom in being soaked to the bone, filthy, and scratched all to hell. Maybe it's because, barring a calamity, things aren't likely to get any worse.

Bob, on the other hand, pointed out that he was a good six inches taller than I am and roughly two hundred years older. It was a lot more difficult for him to get through the route I was taking. Within ten minutes of pushing through the scrub, he refused to go any farther, and we turned around to find another way to our destination.

In chronological years, Bob is only about twenty-five years older. He studied field biology in college before switching to major in wildlife illustration. He did the illustrations for my last book. It's handy being able to cart around your illustrator with you on the road; all you have to do is promise him all kinds of fishing and wild pigs and some adventures.

After wading across what can best be described as a shallow pond and walking a mile or so through marsh grasses, we found what may have once been an access road to the dunes, but which had been flooded by the recent rain. Because we were already soaked, we slogged down the long, narrow marsh into the general area of the tertiary dunes.

The dunes were crisscrossed with pig tracks and signs of their rooting. This is one of the problems with wild swine in a habitat like this; they dig through the dunes to eat sand crabs and the roots of some of the plants that hold the dunes together. The fear is that this action, over time, will lead to the destruction of those dunes and perhaps to the disappearance of the entire landmass into the sea.

It was clear that there had been pigs out here all night. Set yourself up in the dark on one of those ridges with a rifle and a spotlight, and you'd have no trouble knocking the population down. But that isn't allowed, despite the absence of any houses to worry about hitting. I wondered why.

It was a beautiful place. There aren't many spots here on the East Coast where you can walk among the dunes by the ocean without seeing a trace of humans. Instead there were sea oats and raccoon tracks and the thick smell of salt and scrub pines and a touch of honest seaside decay on the wind.

After an hour and a half of ambush and a few attempts to drive any hidden pigs out of the brush and into Bob's line of fire, we packed it in. Hunting pigs in a place like this, in the middle of the day, was turning out to be a fool's errand. As their tracks showed us, once the sun was well up in the sky, the pigs moved down into the same tangled mess of thorns and scrub that had turned us back initially. Visibility in that environment is limited to five or six feet, and it would be impossible to kill the pigs there without baiting them into an ambush.

We were required to check out of the wildlife preserve at the same utility building where we had checked in. I asked one of the rangers if anyone had taken a pig. She said no. A uniformed man whom I hadn't seen before was seated behind one of the folding tables, and he mentioned that someone had brought in a nice deer.

Looking closer at his uniform, I saw that he wasn't with Fish and Wildlife. He looked to be about my age, maybe a little older. I walked over to talk to him.

"Say, are you the biologist here to take samples of the pigs when people bring them in?"

"Yeah, when anyone has one for us. We don't have any yet today."

"What do you look for when one comes in?"

"Any kind of disease that might affect the native wildlife — brucellosis, that sort of thing."

"Well, if you did find a disease like that, what would you do?"

The biologist laughed. "Well, that's the question, all right. We're not really sure. We have a budget to study the pigs, but it can't be used for eradication."

"You're with the USDA?"

"That's right."

"And you're here to help figure out how to get rid of the pigs?"

"We're trying to."

"So what's the plan, aside from the managed hunts like what's happening today?"

"It's just these hunts for now."

"How many pigs do you figure are here right now?"

"Probably about three hundred, just within the refuge borders."

"How many did you kill last year, among all of the hunters you had out here for all of the managed hunts?"

"Fifteen."

"Only fifteen?"

The USDA guy sighed and shrugged. "Yeah, I know. With pigs, we need to be knocking out at least seventy-five percent of the population each year just to keep their numbers steady. They have so many litters every year."

From what Bob and I had just experienced, it wasn't hugely surprising that so few pigs had been killed. By not allowing hunters to check out the territory in advance, the people from Fish and Wildlife were just dropping people off in the dark (literally and figuratively), letting them wander around and essentially educate the pigs. Hunters never had a chance to pattern the pigs or predict where they'd be.

The more I thought about it, the more I imagined how things could be done differently. If the USDA would stop having these big cattle calls that bring out guys like me and just find a few local hunters (as Boca Grande had done in hiring George Cera to deal with their iguana situation), it would be a much better situation. The hunters could be vetted, put through some sort of short ecology course, and given twenty-four-hour access to the property, year-round, with whatever weapons they wanted. Then there'd be hunters who'd get to know where the pigs were at any given time and they could really start killing them.

I mentioned this idea to the USDA guy.

"We can't let people come in here year-round to hunt," he said. "It would be a safety hazard for the researchers."

"What researchers?"

"The people studying the effects of the pigs on the habitat."

When I was in college, fifteen years ago, I actually did fieldwork on the pigs of the Back Bay and gathered data on the damage the pigs were doing to the local ecosystem. I wondered what the USDA still needed to learn after fifteen years that they hadn't already observed. The pigs were clearly a problem and needed to be hunted to keep their numbers in check.

"We don't have much of an eradication budget," the USDA guy said, "but we do have a pretty good budget to study the problem. If we don't use the research budget this year, then we won't get it next year."

Essentially, people couldn't come in to shoot the invasive species, because that would present a danger to the people who were there to study the invasive species. And they couldn't just stop the studies, because then they wouldn't get the money to keep, well, studying it.

As it turned out, the guy was actually a biologist with the USDA, on loan to the state game department for the hunt, and didn't know any of the state hunting regulations. Suddenly it became all too clear why the morning sign-ups were such a mess. The feds had lent their man to the state, and he was now nominally representing the state to the feds as they hashed out state hunting-license issues. Except that none of them had any idea what the others were talking about.

With the logic as this USDA biologist presented it, there was no scenario in which they would actually be willing to kill the invasive pigs. They were there to study the damage the pigs were doing, simply in order to document it. That documentation would be used to obtain more funding to study how bad the problem was. At no point does anyone involved in this process actually make an effort to solve the problem. That would be counterproductive in terms of perpetuating the system. Once you solve the problem, it's no longer there to be studied. Each step, taken on its own, sort of made sense. I could understand how each individual in the system came to do what he was doing in good faith, including the biologist at Back Bay. But as a whole, it added up to policy that seemed to accomplish nothing.

Bob and I changed out of our wet clothes in the brush behind where we had parked the truck. We drove home pondering how the strategy for combating an ecologically dangerous species could have evolved into something this absurd. There had to be a better way to fight feral pigs.

In search of that better way, I got in touch with Daniel Gentry, of Perry, Georgia, and arranged to visit him for a few days to see how they hunt pigs in the South. We'd found him through a friend of a friend of someone Bob discovered in an Internet forum about tractors. Neither of us had ever met the guy, but I'd had a pretty good string of luck with driving hundreds and even thousands of miles to meet up with strangers in order to hunt odd animals.

The leaves on the trees were fiery shades of orange, red, and yellow when Bob and I left home, and as we drove south the fall landscape turned back to summer. The countryside grew greener and the air warmer. Signs for Starbucks disappeared and those for Waffle House took their place. Wisps of Spanish moss dangled from the trees and filtered the light of the setting sun.

We found Daniel's place at around eight at night. I knocked on the door and there he was, ready to go, in his navy blue military-style trousers with a pistol strapped to his hip. He looked to be around twenty years old, thin, lean, and serious. After hellos, he handed me an AR-15 with a night-vision scope. This guy was all business! We walked out back to his fifty-yard range so I could try out the rifle and he could see how I shot.

This is an important ritual among people who are hunting together for the first time. I've worked as a hunting guide and I know the feeling Daniel probably had. When some unknown person shows up to hunt with you, you've got to worry about what he can do with a rifle. You ask yourself, "Does this person know what he's doing? What are his limitations? Will he do foolish, unsafe things with the gun?" A good host or guide needs to find out these things before the hunting starts. Because of this, some type of seemingly informal shooting usually precedes a hunt among strangers. We act as though this ritual is casual and fun, but the reality is that this is an essential test of a newcomer.

As we approached the targets, Daniel stopped short and motioned for Bob and me to stop. I saw something white and round in the grass in front of us. Daniel drew his pistol and fired with lightning speed. The white thing jumped straight up in the air about three feet and then disappeared into the brush.

"What the hell was that?" I asked.

"Armadillo. That's definitely a varmint around here. They go digging holes all over the place. If you see one, you kill it."

We set up our targets and sighted in the night-vision scope on the AR-15. The AR platform is a semiautomatic rifle that was the basis for the better-known M-16 assault rifle used by the U.S. military. Most ARs and M-16s shoot the .223 Winchester cartridge, which is small enough to be illegal in most states to use on deer. It doesn't have enough oomph to do the job reliably.

Most of my hunting experience has been with bolt-action rifles, so the AR felt alien in my hands — heavy and awkward. For someone who spent a few tours of duty carrying a similar weapon in Iraq or Afghanistan, this thing would probably feel perfect. In fact, I know several veterans who have come home from months or years of combat patrol duty and find that their hands and eyes mesh with the workings of an AR more naturally than with any other shooting platform. To me, it felt like shouldering a weed whacker. I wished that I could hunt with one of the deer rifles I'd brought along, but the night-vision scope, which trumped all else, happened to be attached to the AR.

The pigs around Perry are mostly nocturnal. Fortunately, Georgia allows pigs to be hunted at night. In the daylight, you might stumble across one every now and then, but it's not something you can count on. Even in a full moon, it isn't easy to see — and clearly identify — a pig through an ordinary rifle scope. This meant that we would be depending heavily on the night-vision scope.

We started out on foot, working our way around a farm of more than six hundred acres, where Daniel regularly hunts. I am accustomed to checking the wind right away when I start hunting, but Daniel pointed out that when hunting at night, we'd have to keep checking the moon as well. Not only did we need to hunt into or crosswise to the wind in order to keep the pigs from scenting us, but we also needed to avoid having the newly risen moon directly behind us, so that we wouldn't be silhouetted. This was a whole new world of hunting for me.

The world around us was all grays and blacks and whites in the moonlight, which brightened the trees and the sky and the scattered ramshackle farm buildings. We walked single file:

Daniel in front, I in the middle, then Bob. In the dim light of a cloudy moon, we couldn't always see if there was something we could trip over or crunch down on and make an unfortunately loud noise.

"Walk like a cowboy," Daniel instructed.

It was good advice. The fabric of our clothing could also make a noise when we walked with our legs too close together. Walking like a cowboy, with our legs apart and stepping high, we moved more quietly.

We walked a few miles like this in the dark, stopping every so often to scan the fields and pastures for pigs. We crossed over a fence and walked around a small pond, when Daniel and Bob saw, practically simultaneously, a pig-sized black blob. At about fifty yards away, I had an easy shot. I shouldered the AR and lined up the scope. With the night vision, I could see that this was definitely the correct prey.

"You want me to shoot now?" I whispered to Daniel.

"No, wait."

I didn't have the slightest idea why, but this was Daniel's show and I figured he knew what he was doing, or I wouldn't have been there in the first place. I watched through the scope with an itchy trigger finger as the pig trotted away across the field. It crossed the path we had taken, sniffed the ground, and took off toward the woods.

"Why'd you have me hold back?"

"Because that was just the one pig," Daniel said, as if I'd asked something ridiculous. "As soon as we fire a shot, every pig around here is going to disappear for the next four or five hours. You shoot just the one and you aren't gonna get any more."

Daniel was right, in terms of what he was trying to accomplish. I had come to Georgia mostly just wanting to knock out a pig to cook and write about. But Daniel's job as a steward of that land is to remove as many pigs as possible. Sometimes that means passing on the one easy pig in hopes of killing half a dozen at one go later in the night.

We hunted on foot for hours, slowly circling the farm several times. After a while we decided to try another tactic, to cover more ground.

Daniel started his pickup truck with Bob in the cab and me in the bed. He drove out to another farm that he had access to and started driving up and down the access roads. We cruised through enormous fields with massive irrigation systems. I stood up and leaned forward over the back of the cab with the rifle on my shoulder, elbow resting on the roof as I bounced with every rock and bump in the dirt road. The gray-and-white moonlight spectacle of fields and woods flew past as I scanned the tree line with the night-vision scope. I wondered if this was what it was like to be in the Taliban.

We stopped at the end of a long field in front of a gate for which Daniel didn't have the key. As the three of us discussed where to go next, I spied a sizable group of pigs in the next field, on the other side of the gate. There were so many of them, I scarcely believed that this could really be a herd of wild animals. But it was. Thirty or forty pigs all eating in the middle of the field, no more than a hundred and fifty yards away.

With any of my own bolt-action deer rifles, this would have been a simple business. Using a steady rest, I could pick off at least three of them before they were gone. But I wasn't hunting with a deer rifle. I was hunting with an AR-15 that I'd met just that night and shot only at fifty yards. The scope was mounted so high off the barrel that a tremendous amount of holdover would be required for a shot at that distance, as opposed to the fifty yards we'd zeroed the scope at.

Daniel and I whispered in rapid consultation. We had to get closer. The wind was in our favor, at least for the moment. We decided to make an approach from around the tree line at the edge of the field in which the pigs stood.

Bob stayed back at the truck as Daniel and I moved out. We couldn't see the pigs during the first stage of our approach, but we knew where they were likely to be. The moon had sunk out of sight and we dared not turn on flashlights, which would give away our position. We navigated using the trick of looking away from what we really needed to see, shifting our attention to our peripheral vision, which has superior night vision to that of the center of the eye.

This was fine adventure now. The thick Georgia night air was in my nostrils. I felt good and whole and alive as I sneaked up on feral pigs in the dark of night.

When we'd gotten to the point in the tree line that should have put us about thirty yards from the pigs, they weren't there. The herd was on the move, steadily grazing its way down the field. The pigs didn't seem spooked and probably had no idea we were there, but we weren't much closer to them than when we had started.

Faster, we moved down the tree line in pursuit. I saw the leaders of the herd heading straight toward the opening of a trail into the woods on the other side of the long field. The herd was still some hundred and fifty yards away, but this was as good as it was going to get before they were all gone.

I dropped to one knee and brought the heavy beast of a rifle up to my shoulder, resting my left elbow on my knee to steady my aim. My right thumb disengaged the unfamiliar safety switch. I found a pig that wasn't moving at the moment, aimed the low-magnification scope just behind the ear, and opened fire.

All hell broke loose among the pigs. The gun smoke momentarily obscured my vision through the sensitive night-vision scope.

The herd broke into two; some headed straight for the woods, and others ran to the opposite side of the field. One pig, probably the one I had aimed for, was standing still. I fired again, three or four times, peppering both that pig and others near it. And suddenly, with a whole damned herd of feral swine on the move in front of me, the gun jammed.

Have I mentioned how much I dislike hunting with a semi-automatic rifle? I've never once had a bolt-action rifle jam up on me, let alone at such an inopportune moment. Surely it has its place as a hunting tool, and many people swear by them, but this sort of thing makes me think that semiautos just don't like me.

Instantly, Daniel came up behind me. I handed him the rifle and he cleared the jam as quickly as he could. There were still a few pigs in sight and he took a few shots at them himself. Then the herd was gone and we were left wondering what, if anything, we had actually hit.

Pigs are tough. Swine that have gone wild for more than a few generations tend to develop a cape, or armorlike section of hide, over their vital organs. The cape can be up to several inches thick and resists spears, arrows, and even bullets if they aren't moving fast enough or are undersized for the job. When viewed from the side, pigs differ from most other four-legged prey, in the sense that the heart is protected fully by the foreleg. In order to reach the heart or lungs, your bullet must pass through not only the cape but also the whole of that leg's muscle, fat, and bone. This was part of why, at that distance, I had aimed at the neck rather than for the heart.

We walked up to where the pigs had been when we were shooting at them and looked for anything dead. All of them had made it into the brush and woods on either side of the field.

As a deer hunter, my usual rule is that any potentially wounded animal must be followed up on to the ends of the earth, unless a landowner turns me away or the blood trail demonstrates that the animal has been only superficially injured and simply can't be caught up with. Daniel explained that, on this farm, the rules are different with pigs. And I had to admit that his rules made sense.

Daniel Gentry's rule of thumb about following up a wounded pig into thick brush in the middle of the night is that you don't, especially one that's part of a herd of thirty or forty.

Within an open field, it isn't too dangerous to hunt pigs. In the slight but real possibility that a pig heads straight for you, there's plenty of time to get enough bullets into it to stop the charge. Daniel had seen a small herd run straight at him once before. Because he had already emptied the magazine of his AR, it was the 9 mm pistol on his hip that dropped them a scant few paces from where he stood. Usually this sort of thing will happen only if you have the misfortune to be standing directly between the pigs and the nearest cover or woods for them to escape to. Of course, it also happens that Daniel's preferred tactic is to place himself in exactly that position so that the targets get closer and easier to hit once the shooting begins.

Following up on a wounded pig in thick cover is a whole other deal. You aren't likely to see the pig and have a shot opportunity until you're only a few feet away. Keep in mind that these animals typically grow to around three hundred pounds and that they usually have very sharp tusks up to three or four inches long. When you consider that there's an entire herd of them waiting and that they are very angry at you, this is not a situation you should put yourself into without having secured a life-insurance policy that defines the word *suicide* in language that you and your heirs are comfortable with.

It was Daniel's show and we were playing by his rules, so after searching the perimeter of the field for an hour or so, we called off the chase and returned to the truck.

We took a detour on our way out. Daniel steered his truck to the bottom of a gentle hill and parked beside an electric fence. I got out and walked over to the fence to look at what amounted to an open-air graveyard for anything dead on the farm. There were huge cattle skeletons with pelvises that looked big enough to crawl through, and damp masses of gray hair clinging to the desiccated remains of what had been a coyote (a newly invasive species in eastern states). The bones of feral pigs were scattered everywhere. I picked up a lower jaw to which the long fangs were still attached and slipped it into my pocket.

Looking at the size of the boneyard, I asked Daniel how many pigs he'd killed here in the last year.

"About sixty," he said.

Sixty pigs. Killed by one guy, hunting in his spare time, with essentially no budget.

A medium-size boar lay on its side with its mouth open and legs stiff. Shot only yesterday, it was still intact. People don't often eat wild boars; the uncastrated males can have a funky flavor that most people don't like. The shoats and sows are said to make for better eating.

Daniel said he figured this old boy was somewhere between two hundred and fifty and three hundred pounds. I reached out and felt the stiff black bristles on its back. The animal resembled a domestic pig but with a little more hair and a thicker hide than what you'd find in a pigpen. It was black all over.

Judging by their appearance, it's likely that the pigs around Perry haven't been there all that long: just a couple of decades, I would guess. The longer pigs are out in the wild, the more they resemble their wild Eurasian ancestors over the course of generations. The pigs here could be escapees from a commercial pig farm, or perhaps they had been released by people who wanted to hunt them eventually; that happens sometimes. In some cases in which domestic pigs have already escaped to the wild, people have released some wild European stock to interbreed with them. Russian razorbacks are a favorite for this purpose. The pigs I saw around Perry showed no signs of having such blood, fortunately.

The night felt like a success of sorts, even though we hadn't bagged a pig. I'd seen our prey in the wild and been offered a shot, and I knew for sure that Daniel knew what he was doing. We were dog-tired and hungry, and Daniel had a day job to show up for in a matter of hours. We adjourned for the night.

WE GOT TO OUR MOTEL AT DAWN, and Bob and I ate either breakfast or a late dinner, depending on how you figure it at the local Waffle House. Utterly exhausted, I should have gone straight to sleep, but I kept thinking about the armadillo Daniel had taken a shot at. I pulled out my laptop and started doing some homework.

What I found made me want to add armadillos to my hunting list. All nine-banded armadillos found north of the Rio Grande are invasive. Armadillos in the United States can be divided into two distinct populations, on either side of the Mississippi River. On the west side they spread organically from their natural range. As European settlers transformed the landscape through farming, it became more hospitable to the armadillos and they followed this transformation northward. Armadillos have been found as far north as Nebraska, and they continue to expand their range.

Nine-banded armadillos (so named for the nine bands of armor covering their midsection) on the eastern side of the Mississippi descend from a few individuals that escaped from a private zoo in Florida in 1924, when their enclosure was damaged during a storm. The species has been expanding out from Florida ever since.

The armadillo is a cute, dear little creature that invites sympathy, what with its pea-sized brain and all. Even its behavior and its diet seem harmless at first glance. For the most part, it just wants to dig its little burrow and eat grubs, worms, and wasps. An armadillo is very well equipped for digging, with big, broad feet and sturdy claws.

If it kept to its grubs, then perhaps I'd be inclined to let the armadillo go its own way. But armadillos will eat just about any living thing on or in the ground that it can manage. Ninety-five percent of predation on sea turtle eggs in Florida is the work of the nonnative nine-banded armadillo. The eggs and young of ground-nesting birds are at risk of predation by armadillos (and pigs). Ditto for many species of salamander and for the eggs of many other reptiles. As the nine-banded armadillo continues its northerly expansion, there's a long succession of endangered species that could be pushed over the brink of extinction by its arrival.

As I drifted off to sleep, I resolved to get myself an armadillo the next night.

Bob and I woke up and went out for lunch, then came back to our motel room to sleep until a few hours before dusk. We met up with Daniel at his place and I helped him butcher an extremely large deer he'd shot and quartered a few days before.

The Georgian deer was enormous compared to what I had been accustomed to butchering back home in Virginia. This came as a real surprise. There is a concept in biology, known as Bergmann's rule, which describes the tendency for a species distributed widely from the equator toward either polar region to be smaller toward the equator.

This makes sense. When an animal gets bigger, the ratio of surface area (from which heat is lost) becomes lower relative to the total heat-producing body mass. A bigger-bodied animal has an easier time staying warm; a smaller animal loses heat more quickly and avoids heatstroke in a hot climate. In the long run, animals from cold regions, such as those big whitetail deer, will probably either disappear or become smaller when introduced to warmer climates. That said, there are plenty of exceptions to Bergmann's rule — enough that it might better be thought of as "Bergmann's gentle suggestion."

The whitetail buck that Daniel had kept on ice for the last few days represented a pretty big exception to Bergmann's rule, as did every other deer I saw while I was in that part of Georgia. Whitetail numbers crashed between the 1920s and the 1960s, and there were many reintroduction programs around the United States that apparently didn't pay close attention to what subspecies of whitetail was being dropped into which area of the country. Whitetails are native to the United States, but it certainly looks as if at some point a nonnative subspecies from a long way north (probably *Odocoileus virginianus borealis*) was dropped into Georgia. I suppose it was better to have the wrong subspecies than no whitetails at all.

We set out in the truck and cruised in the setting sun, with me bouncing around in the back with my own scoped .30-'06 in my hands. I prayed that we'd see a pig before the sun went down so I could take it with a familiar rifle, but we didn't see anything.

After the sun had set, we went out on foot. We worked the wind and the moon to get over to the same place where we'd seen the lone pig the night before. I quietly explained to Daniel my desire to eat an armadillo, which he thought was absurd but was willing to go along with.

His opinion was that we couldn't shoot it. Or rather we could but we mustn't. The sound of the shot would send every pig in the area into thick cover for the next few hours.

An hour into the hunt, Bob spied the white, oblong form of an armadillo about twenty feet from us, near the edge of a field. Daniel was holding the AR-15, which he handed to me before taking off for the armadillo at top speed. I in turn handed the rifle to Bob and took off running myself, switching on my headlamp as I went.

Imagine a game of soccer in which the ball moves on its own, and you'll have the basic idea of what was afoot: soccer with a moving ball, at night, with headlamps, through a cow pasture. Daniel and I worked the armadillo like a pair of wolves after an elk — steering it where we needed it to go and heading it off away from the woods and thick cover so we would have a chance out in the open.

Armadillos can run surprisingly fast, and for a surprisingly long time. Daniel's idea was that we could run up and kick it in order to stun the creature before finishing it off. This wouldn't work too well, though, because the animal is very well armored.

Although the armor is tough, it's actually not anything like the rigid, bony shell of a turtle; rather, it's made up of scaly plates of something like very thick skin, called scutes. The armadillo has a big scute on each end of its body, with nine smaller ones in the middle, which allow it some flexibility.

The armadillo we were chasing began to tire and slow down, but then so did Daniel and I. Neither of us was really much of a soccer player. Getting low on energy, I decided it was time to plan an endgame. With a final burst of speed, I took a running jump and put a foot down on the armadillo's tail, stopping both of us short. I drew a long, sharp hunting knife from its sheath on my belt and wondered for a fraction of a second how to get through the armor before settling on the base of the neck. In one swift motion, the poor little bugger was dead.

You probably won't get many opportunities to examine the belly of an armadillo, so I suggest you take advantage when a chance comes your way. Curiously, the underside is covered with sparse but thick hairs that give way to scales on the legs. There aren't a whole lot of animals that sport both scales and hair.

I butchered the armadillo within a few minutes of the kill. The process was a bit awkward, what with the armor. The bulk of the meat appeared to be in the hefty hindquarters, so I carved those out and peeled the rear scute from them. I examined the stomach contents and found mostly grubs, a few yellow jackets, and some plant matter that I couldn't identify.

The meat was a rich, deep red that reminded me of white-tail venison. I wrapped up the hindquarters in a plastic bag and placed them in a cooler full of ice. It would take some homework to figure out what to do with them. There is a tradition of hunting and eating them in Central America and a cuisine that goes along with that, but you can't exactly open your ordinary American cookbook to the armadillo chapter and dive right into it.

I've since cooked armadillo a few times, and it's like a cross between chicken and pork. The meat starts out a deep red but turns white as it is cooked. There's nothing wrong with the taste, and in a blind test I think that most people would be fine with it. Yet — strangely, after all the wild animals I've eaten — something sort of gives me the creeps when I'm chewing it. It may just take some getting used to.

Would-be armadillo hunters should be aware that, like human beings, some armadillos can carry leprosy (now often called "Hansen's disease.") The disease is most often found among armadillos close to the Gulf Coast, because of particular soil conditions that foster the bacteria that causes it. Cooking kills the bacteria just as surely as it kills other foodborne pathogens like *E. coli*. And even though ninety-five percent of humans are naturally immune to the disease (and simple antibiotics provide an effective cure), it's still not a smart idea to handle dead armadillos unless you have really done your homework.

We didn't see any more pigs that night, and Daniel had to pack things in by midnight, as he had to be at work bright and early. Bob and I drove back to Virginia that morning with an armadillo but without a pig. Already, though, we were making plans to return to Georgia for another try.

I FINALLY GOT MY CHANCE to cook a wild pig five months later. As one of the few specialists in hunting and eating invasive species, I get a lot of strange e-mail. Some of that correspondence is from random people inviting me to go hunting with them. I've had astoundingly good luck with taking strangers up on their invitations to drive hundreds or thousands of miles to hunt odd things with them in even odder places. It turns out that most people aren't serial killers, and there's little danger in wandering around strange wilderness areas with them while they're heavily armed. Anecdotally, anyway.

This is what happened right about when I needed to bag a pig for keeps. I actually got two e-mails. One was from Kiera Butler, articles editor of *Mother Jones* magazine. She was interested in following along with me on a hunt to find out what this business of hunting and eating invasive species was all about.

The other was a Facebook message from Baker Leavitt, a friend of a former student of mine who had heard about what I was up to. Baker was at that time a resident of New York City but was part-owner of some family property near his childhood home in Georgia. Would I like to "come bust some hawgs!" around Savannah at the earliest possible convenience? Yes, please!

I checked to make sure that it would be okay for Kiera to tag along. She'd never hunted anything, and, in fact, was a longtime vegetarian. (In this, her background reminded me of my own.) As a hunting instructor and guide, though, I was used to working with adults who have no hunting or shooting experience, so this sounded like a situation I could handle.

BOB WAS GAME FOR ANOTHER TRIP, so we made the day's drive together from Charlottesville to Savannah in the dead of February. We checked into our hotel, just outside the city limits, and met up with Kiera. She was a tall, whip-thin young woman who, for a vegetarian from San Francisco, seemed quite eager to kill a pig.

Baker's family's place turned out to be a thousand acres of old rural Georgia standing firm in the face of suburban encroachment all around. We drove into what seemed to be a long-established suburban neighborhood and took a turn into a dirt alley between a few houses, and pretty soon we were back in the country. Stands of live oak were mixed with scrub pines, swampy bottoms, and long meadows that had been carved out of the woods.

Baker is a strong, sturdily built man devoted to the CrossFit movement. (Many of my hunting students have also been part of CrossFit, which is a strength and conditioning program for professional athletes, police, military, and ordinary people.) He spoke rapidly of more businesses he had invested in or started than I could keep track of. Somehow, he was working on an energy-drink company and a sporting-equipment business and a few other projects, all while enrolled in an Arabic-language program at a university in New York City. I imagine he's bound to strike it big in something sooner or later, on odds alone.

Before we hunted, I gave Kiera a crash course in shooting a hunting rifle. We set up an ad hoc range, and I found out what she could do with the 7mm-08 deer rifle that I brought for her. She did well enough for a first-timer, and I figured she'd be all right to seventy-five yards or so. I'd been drilling her on the vulnerable areas of a pig's anatomy for the last few weeks and was confident that she knew which part of the animal to shoot.

Kiera and I walked under a white, threatening sky to our two-person blind. Bob was less than a mile away in a blind of his own. It began to drizzle, but Kiera bore the bad weather with good cheer. We saw many fresh tracks in the area, but no pigs trotted out.

Around midday, we heard several shots from less than half a mile away. I was pretty sure they'd come from Bob's lever-action 30-30 rifle, so we headed back to the dirt road and toward the barn to find out if he'd gotten something.

He had! It was a young boar of around sixty pounds — old enough to have put on some size but still young enough to be free of the "boar taint" (an unpleasant smell to the meat) that is reported in older, uncastrated pigs. We carried it to a wooden platform that was built for the purpose of butchering, and I set to work.

I had never butchered a pig before, so I approached this one in the same way I would butcher a deer. First, I gutted it, noting the various similarities to and differences from deer viscera. Kiera watched with interest and never shied away from what was happening. After it was gutted, Bob hung the pig from a hook and skinned it. (Skinning a pig is, by the way, fairly hard work; the hide is tightly bound to the body compared to how it is with most other mammals.) We put the carcass on ice in a large cooler and did most of the final butchering when we returned home.

In the end, neither Kiera nor I shot a pig on that trip, but we were happy that our expedition was successful and that we had meat to bring home. As far as I know, she's still a vegetarian, but before we parted ways, she carved off a forequarter of her own and cooked it up for dinner.

I DID A LOT OF COOKING with that pig and with other pigs, wild and domestic, that I've killed since. What I found is that the flavor of a wild pig is just about identical to that of a pig raised in the open on a small farm. The difference is in fat content: Domestic pigs put on a lot more fat, which makes for thicker bacon that's easier to cook in the usual ways. There's also more consistency in the size of hams and pork chops from domestic pigs, because they're slaughtered at a specific point in their growth, when they've reached a standard weight. I found no gaminess and no toughness to the meat beyond what happens to any animal as it ages and collagen builds up.

As food, wild pigs are superb. Hunting them takes work and skill, but once a hunter gets to be as good at it as Daniel Gentry is, a lot of mouths can be fed (and wildlife habitat saved).

Lionfish

"I know that if I come back every couple of weeks and kill every lionfish I see, the other fish are gonna come back," Mojo said. "So that's what I do, man. And that's my little corner of the ocean, where we still see the wrasses and the damselfish and the baby grouper and everything else."

My lungs felt as if they would burst as I swam to the back of an underwater cave at the bottom of a cliff. I readied the steel trident in my hand and launched it through the murky water into the body of a reasonably large lionfish. The angry mass of venomous, needlelike spikes twitched and flopped, impaled on my spear. Desperate for air, I swam backward as quickly as I could while trying not to bang my head against the roof of the cave.

Suddenly, just as I was inches from a breath of air, the lionfish managed to wriggle off the end of the spear and dart toward me. Alone and hundreds of yards from the nearest point along the cliffs where I could get out of the water, I wondered whether I would be able to make it out if the lionfish chose to give me a dose of venom.

What the hell had I gotten myself into?

Having gotten a pretty good taste of how invasive species are being dealt with in the United States, I wondered what was happening differently in other countries. This curiosity coincided with coming across the work of Maurice "Mojo" White.

Mojo hunts lionfish around the island of Eleuthera, which is in the Bahamas. He hunts them with an evangelical passion. I think Mojo, an American who's been spending most of the year on Eleuthera diving and surfing since the late 1980s, feels possessive about the reefs: They're *his* reefs, and the lionfish have invaded them.

The lionfish is a species native to the Pacific and Indian Oceans and is so named because of the manelike array of long, venomous spikes extending from its fins. It reaches no more than sixteen inches long, but the lionfish brings trouble out of proportion to its size. Each of those spikes works like a hypodermic needle and is capable of pumping deadly venom into anything that picks a fight with it.

The danger to humans can be compared with that from the bite of a black widow. A lionfish's sting on land isn't usually lethal, but if you get poked while you're handling the fish in a boat or in the kitchen, it's going to ruin your day. Some people are all right within an hour; others describe a blinding pain that rendered them unable even to stand, followed by the affected limb swelling to twice its normal size and a recovery process that lasted months. The effects seem to vary depending on what part of the body is stung, the dose, and whether or not medical attention comes quickly. Only a very few people succumb.

In the water, however, the sting of a lionfish could mean death. If the pain and swelling prevent you from swimming back to land, drowning is on the agenda unless you have a very alert dive buddy.

This was on my mind as I helplessly watched the wounded lionfish decide whether to seek revenge. I was lucky that day. The fish retreated into the underwater cave. I surfaced rapidly, gulping for air.

LIONFISH HAVE SHOWN UP IN THE CARIBBEAN and surrounding waters only recently. It's widely believed that the lionfish were in an aquarium in a coastal Florida home when 1992's Hurricane Andrew smashed it into the ocean, and they escaped into the Gulfstream. This doesn't explain how the lionfish showed up in the waters around Eleuthera some five years ago, but the locals have a theory: They think lionfish eggs were accidentally released to the open water when a high-end resort, boasting what's billed as the world's largest tropical marine aquarium (including a population of lionfish), discharged water from its tanks into the ocean. Apparently, it was only after the resort stocked its tanks with lionfish from the Pacific and Indian Oceans that they also began appearing in local reefs.

The effect of these fish on the reef ecosystem has been rapid and profound. Lionfish will eat just about anything they can fit into their mouth, which isn't unusual for a fish. The trouble is that there isn't much in the Atlantic Ocean that finds them worth fighting. Their deadly weaponry discourages most advances. A big, mature grouper will from time to time suck down a whole lionfish, but lionfish seem to eat a lot of immature grouper and are gradually reducing their numbers. Reefs that were once teeming with a broad variety of life only a few years ago are now almost deserted. In some cases, there's not much left except for lionfish and corals.

Mojo started a blog and a show on YouTube devoted to teaching people to hunt lionfish. *Hunting* is definitely the word for it. It isn't efficient to drop a hook and line and wait for one, as you would with most other kinds of fish. Lionfish hide under rocks, reefs, and other underwater structures, on which a fishing line or a net is apt to snag. They pick a good underwater ledge or alcove and then spend most of their time defending it, and not swimming in open water. You could sit there in a boat all day and not know whether a lionfish was there or if you need go to twenty yards away to the next ledge. The way to really get things done is to get in the water with a mask, fins, a snorkel, and a spear.

After a long phone conversation with Mojo, it became clear that I had to get myself out to Eleuthera to work with him and learn about how the Bahamians are dealing with the lionfish invasion.

I figured it would take two or three days to get what I needed, which meant I had to budget at least a week. That's the funny thing about tropical islands: No one is in a hurry. Ever. Why should he be? The advantage of living on a tropical island in the first place is that things get done when they get done, and maybe they don't get done at all.

The day before I left for Eleuthera, I got a phone call from Mojo informing me that he'd be tied up for a few days in Nassau and wasn't sure when he'd be getting back. This was a bit of a snag in the plan, as I didn't know a soul in the Bahamas other than Mojo, and with nonrefundable tickets I was going to be on that plane the next morning no matter what.

I wouldn't be landing completely cold, however. Mojo arranged for a friend of his, Julian, to rent me a car and to meet me at the airport. The thing is, there are no big rental companies on Eleuthera. If you need a car, it's a question of who you know. Mojo's parting tip before hanging up was that Julian was the fixer. If I needed guns for a goat hunt, information on where to find lionfish, a boat, Julian would be the guy to talk to. Mojo also said that what Julian loved more than any other material thing was venison, which is in short supply on an island with no deer.

Although I was short on money, I had plenty of venison. A whole fridge full, in fact. In the midst of packing, I found time to butcher a couple of hindquarters that I'd been aging from a deer I had shot. I chose the best cuts and prepared them as carefully as I could. I packaged the meat in Ziploc bags, then froze the steaks, roasts, and medallions overnight so that they would stay fresh for the journey.

My first few flights en route to Eleuthera were uneventful, but once I got to Nassau, Delta couldn't get me any farther. Pineapple Air, a local carrier, would take me the rest of the way. I climbed up the steps into a very small prop plane and took one of the few seats.

The cockpit and pilots were right there in front of us, no door or divider. This was handy later in the flight, because I got to watch and listen as various alarms and warnings went off.

Something would start beeping or ringing incessantly and a light would blink rapidly. In every case, both pilots appeared to be ignoring the alarm. I couldn't make up my mind whether to find that reassuring or terrifying.

The ride became turbulent to roller-coaster proportions. I decided not to worry about it too much. My seat belt was buckled, I don't tend to get airsick, and I figured that what with the many islands and cays I could see from the window, it probably wouldn't be too bad a swim if the plane went down in the water.

The plane approached the runway at the North Eleuthera airport shaking, and with some type of alarm going off, as the back end of the plane shimmied in a brutal crosswind. The actual touchdown, though, was surprisingly smooth.

Mine being the only white face in the airport, it wasn't difficult for Julian to spot me. It was a good thing I had someone to drive me around for the first few hours because, as it turns out, the Bahamas are one of those odd places where people insist on driving on the left side of the road. I had been unaware of this fact and, if left to my own devices, probably would have plowed straight into the first oncoming vehicle.

Julian was quiet at first, though later he opened up. He drove me to Mojo's place, where it turned out Mojo's friends from the States, Jon and Jordan, were staying. Jon and Jordan are semiprofessional mixed-martial-arts fighters who came to Eleuthera to surf. Jordan also models and has worked as a paralegal. They'd been on the island for a few days and knew their way around by now. In spite of being extremely nice people, each had a certain predatory air, which made sense for semiprofessional fighters. Their quick eyes reacted instantly to any motion, and they moved with a wary balance, as though they were ready to leap in any direction on a moment's notice and jump-kick someone's chest.

This was a great relief to me; I'm a professional predator myself, and it was good to have people to talk shop with who understand where I'm coming from.

Mojo's house is a classic surf shack that no Hollywood set designer could improve on. Built from whatever materials Mojo could scavenge or repurpose, it resembled Pee-wee's playhouse. Squiggly walkways were built of scrap two-by-fours; lush palms and tropical plants grew over old surfboards stacked haphazardly in odd corners of the yard; weird detritus had been picked off the beach and nailed up wherever it would be useful or decorative. There were pieces of driftwood, mysterious skulls, fan coral, parts of buildings that had been washed into the sea and retrieved. I immediately fell in love with the place.

I dropped my suitcases and Julian suggested a bar where we could get a drink and something to eat. I invited Jon and Jordan to join us, and we left in our respective cars. Julian drove my rental to the Bottom Harbor Beach Club, which, it turned out, he was part owner of. Bottom Harbor was full of American ex-pats, locals, and the odd vagrant surfer. It also had WiFi access. After a couple of drinks, I decided it would be absolutely necessary to become a regular here.

I offer this as tried-and-true words of wisdom: If you find yourself alone in a strange place where you don't know anyone but you've got important things to get done quickly and you're going to need help, find a good bar and show up repeatedly. Buy people drinks with abandon and tip the bartenders lavishly. This is the fastest way to make friends and get information.

Bottom Harbor became my watering hole for the next eight days. Even when it meant going home to eat nothing but hot dogs and stale bread, I showed up at Bottom Harbor and spent money. This ended up being a wise move. Julian and Jon introduced me to a number of people at the bar: Double Dee, an American ex-pat bartender and co-owner of the bar, so named for her massive bosom. Abe and Allie, bartenders and brothers from Oregon with whom I would later go spearfishing.

One night I met a very young Bahamian man named Smith, who wore a red shirt and black pants. Julian and I got to talking to him about drinking and driving on Eleuthera, which is apparently legal and appeared to be almost a national pastime.

"Just don't hit nothing and nobody cares," Smith advised, displaying his melodic Bahamian accent (sort of a Jamaican accent, but softer and with a whole other dictionary of slang). He took a pull on his beer and continued: "Whatever you do, don't get into an accident, especially after dark, mon. You run into something or go off the road out here and you're f**ked, mon. Ain't nobody coming. Go ahead, you call the police. After eight at night, no police officer coming out there. Nobody's coming and you're just f**ked. So don't get into no accidents, mon."

I didn't know if Smith was exaggerating, but the next day I told Jon what Smith had said and asked if there was anything to what the kid had been telling me.

"Smith? You know who he is, right?"

"Not really."

"Smith is the f**kin' magistrate, man. He runs the police department for this whole part of the island."

"That kid looked about eighteen years old! He didn't have on a uniform, just a red shirt and black pants."

"That's how they roll, man. Smitty is all hooked up through his family. I don't know how old he is, but Smitty *is* the law around here. Hell, he was on duty, too."

That first night, I ended up at the octagonal home of a friendly American ex-pat attorney named Sherman, whose wife somehow knew who I was. When it was time to leave, neither Jon, Jordan, nor I had any idea how to get back to Mojo's place. Someone suggested that Julian's shorter and quieter brother, Basil, guide us home.

One of the biggest mistakes of my life was letting Basil drive my rental car. There wasn't much choice, however, given that Eleuthera doesn't have reliable street signs and I had no clue where I was in terms more specific than "somewhere in the Atlantic Ocean."

Anyway, Basil was mind-bogglingly drunk. I suppose that someone driving a car can perhaps swerve a bit or drive extremely fast, but doing both at the same time is really pushing one's luck. I contemplated my own death, and seriously considered opening the door and making a jump for it. After fifteen minutes of the most terrifying journey of my life, much of it spent off the road, Basil let himself out in a town close to Mojo's place. I gratefully took the wheel and followed Jon's borrowed Jeep.

I spent my first full day on Eleuthera driving around with Jon and Jordan in an open Jeep with holes in the floor and a twelve-pack of the local Kilik beer in the back. We met up with Double Dee and the brothers from Oregon and arranged to caravan to the north end of the island to explore some caves. Later, we found ourselves stranded by the side of the road with an overheated engine and a leaking head gasket.

The bad news was that none of us had a cell phone that worked on Eleuthera, and there's no Bahamian equivalent to the American Automobile Association. The good news was that we still had plenty of beer and we were broken down in a tropical island paradise. We applied ourselves to the beer until Double Dee drove up and pulled over to help. Tow trucks are in short supply out there, so we towed out the Jeep with a hemp rope tied to Double Dee's SUV. The day disappeared on us, and plans to get a boat and hunt invasive goats on a nearby island were scrubbed in favor of conch fritters and rum at a wonderful roadside dive.

We stayed up late into the night at Mojo's shack, drinking grog and talking rifles. Sadly, Jon and Jordan had to fly home the next day. Being as close to saints as mixed-martial-arts fighters can be, they left expensive surfboards, board bags, fins, and wetsuits behind at Mojo's place for future visitors to use.

I'd been having a good time so far, but as I drove back from dropping off Jordan and Jon at the airport, I knew I had to spear some lionfish. I drove out to Bottom Harbor to talk to Abe.

Abe is a big, broad man who turned forty the day I arrived on the island. He had wanted to be a physician and had actually started medical school, but left after becoming frustrated with how poorly his patients cared for themselves. He is so agreeable, with such a tendency to be satisfied with the simpler things in life, that it would be easy to assume he's uncomplicated, which would be dead wrong.

Abe offered to go spearfishing with me, but first he had a lot of work to do around the bar, even in the late morning. The kitchen was full of dishes and the bar needed straightening up. I can't bear to sit and watch someone else do all the work, so I ended up spending most of the afternoon washing the previous night's dishes in the kitchen of Bottom Harbor. This wasn't too bad, though, as Abe kept the rum and Coke flowing.

Finally, everything was done. As we considered where to go, Allie, a charter-boat captain, bartender, and real-estate investor, walked in and offered to take us out to a piece of land on the water that he'd recently bought to subdivide and resell. He'd just gotten a road cut out to the water by Julian, who owns and operates a bunch of earth-moving equipment in addition to renting cars and owning a bar. Apparently nobody on Eleuthera does just one thing.

So it was that I found myself clawing my way back to the surface from the underwater cave with a spear in my hand. The lionfish that had slipped off my spear thankfully broke off its pursuit of me and disappeared in the other direction. I took an enormous breath, cleared the fog from my mask, and went in search of another target.

I didn't see the shape so much as the pattern of the lionfish under a rock ledge — a stripy mass of pointy fish flesh. I brought my spear up to the lionfish and readied my aim only a few inches away. Lionfish don't move off even when the hunter is close; they feel that secure about their defensive capabilities. I launched the spear, and the three prongs shot into the fish. It was skewered neatly. I swung the spear about — not too fast, for fear of pushing off the squirming, angry fish. After clearing the ledge and surfacing, I held the spear over the water to avoid attracting sharks and swam back to drop the lionfish into a waiting bucket.

When I'm hunting on land, I feel quite secure. I can tell myself, truthfully, that I'm the most dangerous thing in the woods. Even in the middle of the night, when I'm tracking the blood sign of a deer through thorns and scrub harboring black bears and coyotes and perhaps the odd mountain lion, I believe that. I *know* I'm the most dangerous thing in the forest and, because of that, I'm not afraid. I go forth in the woods with courage and resolve.

Here, in the water, my courage and resolve are muted. It's more a state of moderate willingness and trepidation. Swapping a high-powered rifle for a spear on a rubber band may have something to do with that. Spearfishing in these waters means hunting in the company of massive barracudas and tiger sharks and other things that could rip me open before I could so much as reach for my dive knife. Hunting underwater in the ocean can do wonders for an inflated ego.

I dropped the lionfish into a bucket at the edge of the water and swam out in the other direction along the cliffs. A broad, leopard-speckled stingray flapped its way lazily below. The predator in me readied the spear and wanted to kill it, take it, and eat it for dinner. But I stopped myself midway, knowing that this great beast of five feet in wingspan could kill me in a matter of seconds even if my spear shot true. It happened to Steve Irwin, "the Crocodile Hunter," and he knew what he was doing. Certainly it could happen to me.

Here, I'm not the top predator. That's a hard thing to get through my head. In the ocean, everything I learned hunting in the eastern United States is turned upside down. I'm just so much meat waiting for a fight I can't win.

I nailed another lionfish and brought it up to the bucket. That's when I realized I'd lost sight of Abe. I looked around and didn't see him or a snorkel or any sort of floating thing that might possibly have been Abe.

I told Allie I couldn't find Abe, and we looked for him together from the top of the cliff. Allie climbed to the other side and looked for him there. Many minutes went by. This was bad. If we didn't see him right away, it meant his mortal clock was ticking. He must have gone under one of those rock ledges and hit his head, I thought. Or something else had happened and he was drowning. We had to search the ledges and pull him out and perform CPR and get his heart started before there was serious brain damage, and this had to start *now* because Abe must be out there bobbing in the tide and we *must not* wait any longer. Because Allie was the more experienced diver, I gave him my mask, snorkel, and fins so that he could start searching the ledges while I ran back to the car to get the spare equipment and then could work along the ledges in the other direction.

I thought of Abe with a head injury, bobbing in the tide under a ledge. I wondered if he was still getting air through the snorkel. I thought of the whole journey defined by the sudden death of my diving companion. I thought of Allie and wondered if he would come to hate me for being the reason why Abe was out in the water in the first place. I thought of what would happen when the authorities on Eleuthera came out to determine what had happened. What would this book be in the wake of Abe's death?

Then, Allie called out that he saw something that could be Abe. And it was! Abe was working his way around the point far to our right, way beyond where he should have been. An entire future that had unfolded in my mind suddenly and happily ceased to be.

We brought the lionfish that Abe and I had speared to Bottom Harbor Beach Club in a bucket, more or less alive. We found ourselves shivering, our core body temperature having dropped from being in the water for so long. Shots of Goldschläger warmed us up quickly. The bar filled and I got to talking to a lobsterman named Spider, a strong, wiry, fiftyish man with dark skin and a mostly shaved head — there were just a few thin, razor-manicured zigzags of hair.

Lobstering in the Bahamas isn't done like it is in New England. In the Bahamas, they fish for spiny lobsters, which have no claws. New England lobstermen drop baited traps to the bottom of the ocean and later haul them up on ropes, to be emptied on the deck of a boat. Bahamian lobstermen don masks and fins and dive, holding their breath, with spears. Sometimes they use artificial shelters sunk to the bottom to attract the crustaceans. These are not exactly traps, as the lobsters can leave whenever they want to.

This method shapes the experience of the fishermen in several ways. First, it makes them total badasses. Second, they have a very good idea of what's happening on the reefs. They see with their own eyes the diversity and density of species on one reef as opposed to on another, and they know when things are changing, for better or for worse.

"I know the lionfish is the enemy of the grouper," Spider said, not a trace of doubt in his voice.

"You mean the lionfish eats the baby grouper before it gets big?"

"Yes. But the grouper, when he is big, he swallows the lionfish whole and sucks him right in."

Spider had been diving for lobster around Eleuthera for a long time, and he had been observing changes. I thought about what I had seen in the water that day and realized that most of the fish bigger than a few inches had been the invasive lionfish. There were some barracuda chasing the little baitfish, that stingray, and a few blue tangs, not much else.

I asked Spider if he'd ever eaten lionfish, and he told me they were very good. Because we happened to have a bucket full of them, I invited Spider to show us how to cook them.

In the kitchen, he plucked a lionfish from the bucket with a pair of tongs and set it on its side on a cutting board. He clipped off the venomous fins with sturdy shears, but pointed out that we still needed to avoid the clipped-off ends.

A dull fillet knife was produced. Spider deftly carved around the back of the head and straight down behind the gills, to the bone. He worked the knife backward along the skeleton from this cut and pulled off the fillets without gutting the fish.

Spider called for some vinegar, lime juice, and salt. He mixed these in a bowl with water and soaked the fillets to produce a sort of ceviche. The lionfish was good prepared this way, but not amazing.

Following Spider's method, Abe and I took turns carving up the other lionfish. Although I'm always interested in learning the local way of butchering anything, I thought there might be a more efficient way to get the maximum amount of meat from these smallish fish. Quite a bit of food was left on the discarded carcasses. How about if we scaled and gutted them; dressed them with a bit of lime juice, pepper, and olive oil; wrapped them in grape leaves; and roasted them whole, Greek-style? I like cooking largemouth bass and crappie this way at home, usually over a smoky hardwood fire.

Because Abe had cooked lionfish before, I let him prepare it the way he usually would. He cut the fillets into bite-sized pieces, then mixed up a batter into which he dunked the chunks before frying them in oil.

The result was superb. Each piece of flaky, soft fish melted in my mouth. This was really worth the work we'd put into getting the fish. Fresh and hot, straight from the sea and kitchen, this was a dish that could be pursued with the passion my Massachusetts-born mother reserves for fried clams.

Clearly this stuff had promise. Unfortunately, we'd cooked all of the lionfish, and I hadn't been able to taste it in a simpler, unadorned state. I was going to have to get more.

THE NEXT DAY, around noon, I found myself feeling queasy. Within a few hours, I was curled up on the floor, in the dark, in the fetal position. I was dizzy and had some mild hallucinations: a mistaken impression of movement continually registered in my peripheral vision. I would look to see what had been moving and nothing would be there. It was somewhat more disconcerting than it needed to be, as there were tiny lizards running around, both indoors and out. Every now and then I would look over at my "hallucination" and see a little green lizard pouncing on something next to my head. Well, the lizards were probably there, but I can't say for sure . . .

Nobody else who had eaten the lionfish became sick, and my progression of symptoms matched up with the accounts of people who had accidentally drunk some of the tap water at Mojo's place. Hmm. At Mojo's place the night before, after doing all that washing, I'd drunk out of a glass before it had fully dried. That must be it, I figured.

I woke up on my last full day on Eleuthera to a man's voice bellowing from the front gate. I pulled on a pair of jeans and stumbled down the walkway, rubbing my eyes against the sun.

A kind-looking, middle-aged surfer named Rat Dog explained that he'd gotten word from Julian that Mojo and someone named Joey were finally flying into Eleuthera at noon, and that I needed to pick them up at the airport. I felt more or less recovered and up to the job. Today was my last chance to hunt lionfish on Eleuthera, and no matter what, I needed to get Mojo and convince him to head for the water with me right away.

With the combination of luck and intrepidity of an old Caribbean hand, Mojo had managed to get a free ride for himself and Joey from Miami to Nassau on a mega-yacht being delivered by a jobbing captain to its new owner. From Nassau he'd done his best to hop to Eleuthera on one boat or another, but had finally punted and taken a commercial flight on Pineapple Air.

Joey was a very young, whip-thin surfer with long blond hair and a perpetually optimistic and buoyant outlook. Mojo turned out to be much as he appeared in his YouTube videos: a middle-aged surfer in excellent shape after decades of riding the waves. He slipped on reading glasses when nobody was looking, but he spoke like the stereotypical surfer.

"Back again," Joey repeated several times, staring out the car window and shaking his head. These two fixtures of Eleuthera had been in the United States for months. Old stomping grounds waited to be reclaimed.

We drove to Mojo's place to pick up gear. I grabbed the wetsuit Jordan had left behind and crammed myself into the undersized rubber contraption.

After more than a week of waiting for Mojo to show up, it felt surreal for him to be sitting in the car beside me. By now I thought I had a pretty good handle on what the lionfish situation was around Eleuthera. I knew how to find and spear them, and I was sold on the flavor. What I didn't quite get was how Mojo's approach was any different from that of any of the other people involved in lionfish-catching tournaments in the Atlantic.

We drove around looking for a good spot with favorable tide, swell, and wind for diving. I found myself repeatedly turning off onto vegetation-choked access roads, bouncing over potholes that even a Jeep would have winced at, and coming to dead ends or finding that the water wasn't quite right. As we explored, Mojo explained his approach to the lionfish problem.

"We can't get them out of the ocean. They're probably here to stay now," he said. "But you know, a lot of these fish that are in trouble because of the lionfish don't need the whole ocean to survive. I've got my little spots and patch reefs where I dive, and those are *my* reefs, man. And I know that if I come back every couple of weeks and kill every lionfish I see, the other fish are gonna come back. So that's what I do, man. And that's my little corner of the ocean, where we still see the wrasses and the damselfish and the baby grouper and everything else."

Mojo was on to something. The conventional response to invasive species has been either to shrug or to assume that, in order to accomplish anything, the species must be eradicated from its new environment through a massive control program. What Mojo was doing was something on a much smaller scale that could still have a profound effect. This finger in the dike could be the difference between extinction and survival for many Atlantic species. If a few diligent volunteers like Mojo were to accept responsibility for a short stretch of coast and remove most of the lionfish on a weekly basis, maybe there'd still be places where other fish could survive. Maybe fish from the deeper ocean could come to have the cleaner wrasses remove their parasites and extend their lives. Maybe there would still be a place where grouper fry could mature into adults.

The difference between a thousand survivors and zero is profound, even for a species that once counted in the millions.

Getting people to accept responsibility for the environment takes some evangelizing, though. After a day of fishing, Mojo makes a habit of cleaning his lionfish in front of people. Even if it would be easier to do it right there on the beach, he finds a pier or someplace where a bunch of locals can see what he's doing. They invariably express shock and tell him that the fish are poisonous and that he shouldn't touch them. This creates an opportunity for Mojo to show them where the venom is and how to safely remove the spines and prepare the fish as food. In this way, he encourages as many people as possible to eat lionfish, and thus to create a demand for it.

Volunteers with spears and snorkels can do a lot to clear lionfish out of an area. Commercial lobster divers, already in the water with spears in hand, can do even more. Give them a good price per pound, on par with what they're getting for spiny lobsters, and they'll be spearing lionfish in great numbers.

This isn't a recipe for eradication, but perhaps it's a recipe for survival.

WE PULLED UP TO A SHORT ROCKY BEACH on an inlet in the tiny hamlet of Alicetown. This would do, Mojo decided. We donned our gear and waded into the water.

At first, the going was easy. I could stop swimming and stand up against the rock wall we were swimming along. But there were no lionfish, so we swam farther out, to some submerged rocks that Mojo thought would harbor some. This was where a very important fact asserted itself: I have no real ability as a skin-diver, and I go swimming no more than once every two years.

I finally understood the real value of a wetsuit. Not only did it keep me warm during prolonged sessions in the water, but its buoyancy also helped keep me from drowning. I was in no way prepared for the physical rigor of swimming and treading water in the ocean for more than an hour while trying to find (and film) lionfish. To boot, there was a pretty good swell coming in once we got past the point of land that shielded the inlet. As experienced surfers, Joey and Mojo had little trouble. I was mostly trying not to drown. The water was deeper here, and the lionfish deeper, too, than they had been during my previous hunt. I could see how practicing holding your breath makes a difference in how long you're able to stay under.

The three of us collectively nabbed half a dozen lionfish and three or four spiny lobsters, Joey and Mojo accounting for most of the catch. Mojo came up with a trick for storing lionfish far out from shore or a boat. He'd picked up a dry bag of the same type I'd used many times while canoeing, but instead of using it to keep things dry, he put just enough water in it to keep a few fish alive and then filled the rest of the bright yellow bag with air before sealing and fastening it shut. The bag floated on top of the water and we could easily tow it. It was made of tough enough material that lionfish spines couldn't puncture it (or us) and at the same time it kept both the blood and the vibrations of an injured fish from reaching the keen senses of sharks. Instead of having to swim hundreds of yards to shore every time we speared a fish, we were able to stay out and keep hunting.

After an hour or so, I reached a dangerous physical breaking point. I was starting to really shiver and was gradually losing the ability to keep swimming. There's no question that spearfishing requires athleticism. I told Mojo and Joey that I was heading back in. Joey joined me. Although he's a stronger swimmer than I'll ever be, having roughly two percent body fat caused him to lose heat in the cold water even faster than I had.

Onshore, Joey shook uncontrollably. I started the car, turned up the heat, and had him sit inside while we waited for Mojo. On his way in, Mojo had managed to wrangle up two more lionfish that I'd obliviously swum past only minutes earlier, including one that was in water less than waist deep.

That's the aspect of spearfishing for lionfish that, ironically, makes it *less* dangerous than, say, playing in the surf. Anyone who lives near an invasive population of lionfish (which now run all the way up the east coast of North America as far as the Outer Banks of North Carolina) is already at risk of stepping on one or brushing up against it and getting stung. To go from swimming in that water to actually hunting lionfish is, if anything, an improvement. The lionfish hunter is actively looking for lionfish, and taking great pains to keep the creature on the opposite end of a long stick.

A quick shinny up a coconut tree (it chafes, I discovered) and a hatchet blow later, and Joey and I were guzzling coconut water to replenish our electrolytes. Then it was time to return home and cook our catch.

BACK AT MOJO'S, we filleted a couple of lionfish and Mojo cooked them very simply in a pan with nothing more than a little olive oil and lemon pepper. (He's a fiend for lemon pepper; I counted seven little jars of the stuff in his spice cabinet.) At last, I was able to taste the more or less unadorned flavor of lionfish, without any fried dough or other possibly disguising accoutrements.

The sun had gone down and the kitchen in Mojo's pleasant wood shack was lit by the warm glow of a couple of bulbs. The cooked fish was white and firm, looking much like good cod or sea bass. I took a bite.

The flavor was clean and bright. The firm texture was reminiscent of that of Chilean sea bass. Very good. Nothing "fishy" about it. This stuff could credibly appear on the menu of any high-end restaurant. In fact, lionfish has it all: flavor, texture, environmental responsibility, and a dash of romance — the knowledge that a diver had to risk a hit from the venomous spines has got to add to its marketing panache.

That night I lay in bed looking up at the wooden ceiling of Mojo's shack, thinking that if food writers would promote the fish, and if wholesalers, fishmongers, and chefs would order it and put it in front of diners, then lobstermen like Spider would spear them in quantity. People like Mojo would teach them how to handle the fish safely. The continuous chain of refrigerated shipping from the Bahamas to the United States is already there to support trade in spiny lobster, conch, and grouper. All of the pieces of a system to clear out the lionfish en masse on a commercial scale are right there just waiting to be brought together.

Until those elements are linked, though, Mojo's belief in accepting personal responsibility for the problem is making just a small difference — but a real one nevertheless.

European Green Crabs

WITHIN DAYS of returning from Eleuthera, I did a phone interview with James Gorman, of the *New York Times,* for an article he was writing about the concept of eating invasives. I'd been working on this book full-time for several months and had also been blogging about the idea. At this point I was, as far as I knew, the only public advocate for eating invasive species as a systematic response to their threat.

Gorman coined a term to describe those who espoused the concept: invasivores. At first I wasn't keen on the word but, on further reflection, I realized Gorman was right. This whole thing really needed a unique name to describe it.

As a result of the official name, people got the impression that I was part of an invasivore *movement.* I started receiving all sorts of e-mails and interview requests about the "movement." In reality, there was no movement. It was just me, driving around, killing weird things, and eating them. As Arlo Guthrie says in "Alice's Restaurant," greatly abbreviated: It takes three people to make an organization and fifty to call whatever you're doing a movement.

After a while, though, it became self-fulfilling. People all over the country asked me for advice about how to hunt iguanas or starlings or whatever other invasive animal was in their area. Other bloggers began writing about it. Somehow a nascent movement actually took shape.

Discovering the potential for putting lionfish on restaurant menus got me excited about creating markets for invasive species as food. After Gorman's piece in the *Times,* I received good feedback from chefs and foodies about the prospect of putting a price tag on certain species. The biggest barrier to selling most invasive creatures as food here is the maze of U.S. Department of Agriculture and U.S. Food and Drug Administration paperwork and regulations — specifically, the requirement that most species be killed in an approved slaughterhouse rather than in the field. The exception is seafood. Fish can be killed on the boat and still be sold as food. I figured I ought to take a look at what else was in the ocean near American shores that could be rounded up in large quantities and sold without legal hassles.

European green crabs seemed to fit the bill. *Carcinus maenas* is a small crab that has increasingly dominated portions of the east and west American coasts since its accidental introduction in the early 1800s. It's thought to have been brought to American shores from Europe in the ballast tanks of ships. Also known as a littoral or shore crab, it's incapable of swimming to the top of a bucket of water, let alone across the Atlantic Ocean, without human intervention. Shore crabs are unfussy omnivores that will eat many types of plants and any animal protein they can scavenge, including oysters, small fish, and other crabs.

I have a vivid memory of what must have been European green crabs from when I was five years old. My family was staying in a house on the coast of Maine for the week, and every day my brother and I would climb around the rocks at low tide, gathering mussels that our father steamed for dinner. One morning, while looking for mussels, I stopped to watch a drama unfold among a group of crabs.

A large crab, about the size of my hand, was engaged in a battle under a few inches of water with five much smaller green crabs. I thought the larger crab would surely win right away, but the smaller crabs kept up their attack. One of them got onto the big crab's face while another had him from behind. One of the big crab's legs was severed and things were generally not going his way when my mother called my brother and me back to the house.

In hindsight, those smaller green crabs must have been the European invaders. Through their tenacity, numbers, and willingness to eat whatever presented itself, they were beating down that larger native crab just as surely as they have dominated most of the East Coast north of the Chesapeake Bay. Commercial fishermen don't like them because they're believed to kill and eat young Dungeness crabs. They also drastically reduce clam populations. The town of Edgartown, in Massachusetts, decided the crabs were causing so much harm to the native scallop population that it implemented a bounty program. The town offered forty cents per pound of the crab. Many tons were removed, most of them to the landfill, and the scallop population recovered.

Bounty programs can work well, up to a point. The problem is that once the invasive's population has been decreased significantly, it becomes more trouble than it's financially worth for bounty hunters to go after the survivors. Most invasive species can bounce back from a tight population bottleneck — after all, that's how they came to be successful invasives in the first place. Even a good bounty program usually ends up being a cyclical effort that constantly costs money and tries the patience of legislators and program directors with other budget priorities. A species balloons out of control, the bounty hunters reduce it, and then they ignore the species for a few years, until it starts getting out of control again.

Often, government entities believe they have to choose between a bounty program that pays by the pound or head and hiring salaried hunters and trappers as government employees. The best approach might be to use both but at different times. Let the bounty hunters clear out the species in large numbers. Once they've taken out all of the low-hanging fruit, bring in experienced specialists on salary to hunt the ones that had been out of reach. The last of any invasive species are always the most difficult to get rid of — after all, they managed to *be* the last — and the value of removing the final five percent is arguably much greater per animal than is that of the first ninety-five percent.

The ideal would be to create a commercial market for an invasive species rather than budgeting public money for bounties. But would anyone really want to eat European green crabs?

This was what I had to find out.

THE TRICKY THING IS that most shore crabs are pretty small. A big one can be up to four inches across — approaching the dimensions of a medium-size blue crab. Picking crabmeat is a tedious job, even on larger crabs. I wondered if there was a way of getting the meat out efficiently enough to make the crabs worth bothering with.

Once again, the *New York Times* stepped into the story. I read an article in the *Times* that mentioned a restaurant called Miya's Sushi, in New Haven, Connecticut. In addition to having this country's biggest selection of vegetarian sushi, Miya's was lauded by the *Times* for serving invasive seafood. That got my full attention.

I looked up Miya's menu online and found that the owner, Bun Lai, had included European green crabs. Now I was really interested. I immediately decided to make the four-hundred-thirty mile drive to New Haven.

Bun and I exchanged e-mails about his restaurant and about the crabs. He would be in San Francisco for a while, but he offered to put me in touch with his crab supplier. Oysterman Brendan Smith was catching crabs on the side for Miya's, and we arranged to meet at the restaurant.

A couple of days later, I found myself walking a few blocks from Yale University to Miya's, pleasantly surprised at being just five minutes late after nine hours behind the wheel of a car. It was a little before dusk.

I could see that Bun had put a lot of thought into the diversity of his menu. There were cheap drafts of Pabst Blue Ribbon and five-dollar California rolls for students eating out on a small budget, but there were also high-dollar adventures in seafood for serious foodies. Miya's is a place where all sorts of people feel welcome: vegetarians, carnivores, . . . and, apparently, invasivores as well.

Brendan Smith (who goes by "Bren") is not your usual oysterman. Bren had a good career in law and worked on Capitol Hill for a while. He could have easily made good money at a large firm, or in a lobbying outfit, or working for a public-interest group. Somehow, though, the fishing life kept calling to him. Even when he was living in a small apartment in Washington, DC, he experimented with aquaculture in large plastic storage tubs. It didn't work out, and most of the fish died quickly.

Years later, he gave aquaculture another go, this time in Long Island Sound as an oysterman (there were also some stints as a lobster fisherman in Massachusetts and as a long-line fisherman on the Bering Sea). Modern American oystermen don't usually just dredge up oysters. Many of them are putting as much effort into seeding oyster beds as they are in harvesting them.

Within half an hour, Bren had convinced me that the best and most ecologically sustainable food in the world is the oyster. (Maybe the pitcher of beer had something to do with my agreement.) Oysters are the lungs of an estuary. The more of them that you seed, the healthier the bay or sound tends to become. Each female produces many millions of eggs. In a laboratory setting without predation, it's common for two of the mollusks to produce millions of seed oysters and replace a substantial annual harvest by humans.

Through the disruption of complex predator–prey relationships, shore crabs end up being bad for oyster numbers. The constant reseeding of beds by oystermen like Bren is one way of countering this problem. Direct removal of the crabs is another.

A few courses into our sushi, the waiter brought out the main attraction. To my surprise, we were presented with a flat rock as a serving platter. On it was a sliced sushi roll artfully arranged. Perched atop the sushi were half a dozen steamed green crabs, whole, and arranged in a lifelike fashion.

It looked magnificent. But what were we supposed to do with the crabs? Were they garnish, the crustacean equivalent of a parsley sprig?

No, Bren assured me. These crabs were meant to be eaten. Whole. They'd been steamed and seasoned with a special combination of spices Bun had concocted.

I doubtfully lifted a crab, its hard shell intact, put it into my mouth, and started chewing. It wasn't bad. I half expected a mouthful of chipped teeth, but the shell was so thin that it crunched right down, like a spicy crab potato chip. As with a potato chip, I couldn't eat just one. I really wanted more.

What Miya's had was the perfect bar food. If you put a bowl of these on a bar as you would potato chips or pretzels, people wouldn't touch them at first. After a few drinks, though, guys would dare each other to eat one and then they'd discover that they're really good. Eventually, you'd be selling them by the hundred instead of by the half dozen.

I got to wondering how Bren had been catching the crabs. He told me he'd been able to supply Miya's needs easily, simply by walking around in tide pools at low tide, picking up crabs, and putting them in a bucket. One trick he recommended was to bury a bucket in the sand with the top level with the surface of the sand. Let the tide come in, then check the bucket when the tide ebbs. Shore crabs tend to fall into the water-filled bucket but can't swim out or climb the smooth sides. Any baited trap that catches blue crabs will also work for shore crabs, Bren said.

"When exactly did you and Bun decide to catch shore crabs and put them on the menu?" I asked.

"Last winter," he said. "Bun's always been a serious conservationist and puts things on the menu that are sustainable. But there was something he saw in the *New York Times* about eating invasive species, and he jumped right on it."

Huh. Small world!

By the end of the evening, I was sold on the crabs as food and was ready to find some in the wild. Bren suggested a nearby state park on the water, where the crabs should be plentiful and I could legally gather as many as I could catch.

The next morning, I drove a few miles from my motel to the park, which is on the Connecticut side of Long Island Sound. I walked across a long boardwalk over the mudflats that ran between the parking area and the beach. Below the railing, there were twenty or so crabs visible for every square yard of mud. Two species appeared to dominate: some species of fiddler crab and the invasive shore crab.

A good method for catching crabs here is to take a long string or a length of fishing line and tie a chicken neck or some other scrap of meat to the end. Tie the other end to the railing and throw it down onto the mudflat. In ten minutes, the bait will be crawling with crabs, which will hold on to it even as you pull up the string and shake off the crabs into a bucket. Blue crabs are often caught from the water by the same method.

I walked to the beach and into the tide pools around the rocks and short stone jetties. At first I didn't see any green crabs in the tide pools. Then I started turning over rocks and found them hiding. The trick was to scoop them up with both hands, each hand closing in from a different side so that they scoot away from the one hand and into the other. Their little claws didn't pinch enough to do me any harm.

My hope was to gather up a good half gallon of the crabs and have enough to bring some home. But I had made a mistake that no experienced fisherman would: I ignored the tide. The surf began to roll in soon after I began my walk, flushing out the tide pools and gradually merging them with the open water.

I enjoyed the walk along the Sound a little longer. A couple of white egrets paced the edge of the mudflats, probably hunting the same crabs I was. Red-winged blackbirds stopped on fence posts and cocked their heads at me. Joggers along the boardwalk looked at me like I was an idiot: a grown man with his jeans rolled up to his knees, wading in tide pools and playing with crabs. I'm accustomed to those looks. . . .

Back near the parking lot, there was a picnic area with heavy iron grills set into the ground. I retrieved a bag of charcoal from my trunk and supplemented it with some driftwood. Once the fire was going, I set a pot with a bit of water in it on the grill and tossed the dozen or so crabs in to steam. I had nothing more than hot sauce, lime juice, salt, and pepper to season them. Old Bay Seasoning would have been nice.

The result was edible, though not nearly as good as the crabs served at Miya's. Keeping them alive for a few hours, to enable them to purge anything from their digestive system, would no doubt have improved the flavor. But this was definitely a food source that could be exploited simply by walking along the beach.

On your plate, shore crabs are a more challenging thing to contemplate putting in your mouth than is, say, a lionfish fillet. But going for a walk on the beach or dropping a few strings onto a mudflat is a lot easier and less dangerous than spearing a lionfish. Gathering shore crabs was possibly the easiest hunting I've ever done.

Asian Carp

Big silvery torpedoes of some twenty pounds launched themselves out of the water as high as ten feet in a fast graceful arc right into the middle of the boat. They smacked into the aluminum and flopped around in bloody confusion as I tried to pounce on one, even as another came hurtling in.

ASIAN CARP HAVE BECOME a sore point for me over the past year.

On my parents' property, in rural Virginia, there are two ponds. I grew up in that house from the age of thirteen and spent many a day on those ponds, fishing and observing the wildlife. I knew everything that lived in each pond: the snapping turtles and bullfrogs, muskrats and fish, the stonefly larvae and the various aquatic plants. Pond ecology is a tidy thing to study up close — a small system, but often a complex one nonetheless.

One day in early autumn, shortly after returning from my trip to hunt invasive lizards in Florida, I walked to the lower pond and saw something highly improbable. An enormous fish that looked to be about three feet long was basking, clearly visible, just beneath the surface. Nothing that belonged in a Virginia pond in the foothills of the Blue Ridge Mountains could grow anywhere near that size.

At first, my fisherman's heart thumped at the sight of a fish that big. But then I gradually realized what it probably was. A carp. A nonnative fish, which some reckless fool must have dumped into the pond.

Further observation suggested that there were around a dozen of the fish there. They spooked easily, rolling in the water and slapping it, almost like a beaver would, when I approached. The pond was mostly barren of plants and had turned a brown, muddy color. It was no longer the healthy ecosystem I had grown up watching.

I asked my parents if they knew where the fish had come from. They asked around, and it turned out that neighbors had stocked the pond with grass carp for the purpose of combating the duckweed, which they thought unsightly. Considering that they owned only a few yards of frontage on the pond and that Virginia law requires the signed consent of all landowners before stocking a pond or lake with carp, what they did was, in fact, illegal.

The carp had to go; the question was how. The neighbors threatened me with unspecified consequences if I removed "their" carp from our pond. I rather enjoyed the thought of what would unfold if they called the game warden to complain about my fishing for carp on my family's land, in a pond that they had illegally stocked.

There are four species of invasive carp in the United States. The one I encountered in the family pond was the grass carp. Grass carp are native to Asia and were brought to this country in the 1960s for aquatic-weed control. They're very successful in this role; they'll eat just about any old plant.

The trouble is that carp don't have any idea of when enough is enough. They keep eating long after they've eaten the weeds they were brought in to control. Often the surface weeds aren't their first choice, and it's only after wiping out most of the important native aquatic plants that they get around to eating the things people are trying to get rid of.

This has obvious consequences for the rest of the ecosystem. Removing native plants means they're not available as a food source for other aquatic herbivores. Also, the plants are no longer providing cover for smaller fish and invertebrates, increasing the amount of predation on them by other species and gradually reducing their numbers. These changes produce a domino effect that creates other ecological problems.

Once the easy food is gone, the carp need to root around for more. Their constant search stirs up sediment that clouds the water. This decreases the amount of light reaching the bottom and further impedes growth of the aquatic plants necessary for the healthy functioning of the pond ecosystem.

Unfortunately, human beings tend to be more concerned with the aesthetics of nature than with its health. A surface covered with scum may not be the best thing for a pond, but dumping a bunch of heavyweight fish that can grow up to fifty pounds will eventually make things worse. State governments have recognized this, and in most places it's now illegal to introduce viable — that is, able to reproduce — grass carp into the wild.

Nonviable carp, on the other hand, are sometimes stocked. Grass carp can be made to be triploid through artificial means. A triploid grass carp has an extra set of chromosomes that cause it to be sterile. This condition is usually induced by spinning the eggs in a centrifuge very quickly and then stopping; the rapid change in pressure naturally results in the extra chromosomes. Triploid carp are considered safer for weed control because they can't reproduce and get out of control.

Although they can't reproduce, they can still wreak havoc for years on the water system they've been introduced into. And even when triploid carp are purchased in good faith, there's no guarantee that they are, in fact, what they're advertised to be.

Carp breeders are known for being meticulous about ensuring that all the fish they sell are unable to breed. Many of them test every single carp before making a sale. Not every egg turns out triploid, and success rates for a batch range from eighty to one hundred percent. There's decent government oversight of the breeders, and they're seldom a problem. The middlemen who buy from the breeders, however, are somewhat of a mixed bag.

Carp expert Duane Chapman, of the United States Geological Survey, let me in on a little secret about triploid grass carp: They aren't always triploid. The value of a standard grass carp is much lower on the market than that of a triploid grass carp. An unethical middleman may buy a certain quantity of certified triploid grass carp and a larger amount of standard grass carp. In the event of an inspection, he presents the certification for the triploids. In that way, he sells the standard carp fraudulently as triploid. The total sales figures are obscured, and it's unlikely the transaction will be questioned by the authorities. Even if fraud is detected, it can be very difficult to build a case.

As you can see, stocking what are believed to be sterile, triploid grass carp isn't guaranteed. Viable carp are being introduced to the wild via the triploid exception. If there's any route by which the carp can escape from a pond into moving water, which is what they need in order to spawn, trouble is around the corner. Even when a drainage stream looks too small for the carp to escape through, this can change rapidly with a heavy rain.

Even when stocked carp are definitely triploid and don't pose a risk of escaping and breeding in the wild, they still wreak havoc on the pond ecosystem they're introduced into. The fish are often stocked when they're about twelve inches long. Say that twenty carp are stocked. A year later, the weeds are gone and the carp might be twenty inches long. But they keep getting bigger. In another year those twenty carp might be thirty inches long. They're having a bigger effect on the habitat every year. If the desired effect (weed removal) was already achieved, then, rationally, the number of carp should be reduced. There's no need to keep a thousand pounds of carp rooting around in the pond if half that biomass was doing the job the year before.

I began experimenting with various fishing methods for the grass carp in my family pond. At first I tried hooks baited with corn, which many people swear by. The fish weren't the slightest bit interested. Even when I chummed an area with it and came back the next day, the corn was untouched. Next I tried ambushing them with my cast net, ready to throw it over a fish as soon as it came within range. Carp are just too wary and pay too much attention to what's happening above the surface for that to work. They were always out of the path of the net by the time it hit the water.

Maybe snagging them would work. In warm weather, carp like to bask at the surface. While bass fishing, I discovered that I could cast over a fish's back from far away and it wouldn't react to either the lure or the hook sliding over it. Now, I bought the biggest treble hook I could find and tied it onto an eighteen-pound test line on my heavy surf rod with a weight under it. Just my luck: the temperature dropped right when I did this and the carp stopped basking.

I was running out of ideas on how to clear out these carp when I drove to Connecticut to try the shore crabs. My cousin Patrick McNamara lives only a few hours away in Massachusetts, and he is a diehard fisherman. The man compresses a five-day work week into four twelve-hour shifts in order to have three solid days to fish. He's been known to sit on a beach in freezing rain for days on end to catch a run of striped bass. If anyone could help me break my losing streak on carp, it was Patrick.

From Connecticut I drove to Wilmington, Massachusetts, with one quick stop at a tackle shop. Within minutes of my arrival, Patrick suggested we try to catch the evening bite in a trout stream a few minutes away. I don't think I'd even dropped my backpack from my shoulder. I'd come to the right place.

We hit the trout stream and took home a few nice rainbows. I had just finished gutting them when he had me back in the car to go fish for eels and bullhead catfish on Silver Lake — in the dark. The next morning we drove to the Concord River to a spot Patrick promised was loaded with carp.

His friend Justin Torname came along. We brought our heavy surf rods in anticipation of heavy carp. I also brought one of Patrick's much lighter spinning rods, in case there was anything else to fish for.

Patrick's bait of choice was oatmeal. I didn't see how it would stay on the hook, but it was a simple matter to roll the stuff into a little ball and slip it onto the hook. Even underwater, the ball held together for a long time.

Patrick had the first bite. He grabbed the rod from its holder in the riverbank and started muscling in the fish. The rod was bent over so far that I thought it would break. Within a few minutes, he'd fought the thirty-inch fish to shore. Justin scooped it up with my landing net.

Seeing a new species up close and personal is always amazing to me. This fish had a yellowish face and a downward-oriented mouth with a couple of short barbels (small protrusions on the lip). What we were looking at was a common carp, not a grass carp. Not the same species, but close enough to get excited. Common carp are native to central Europe and are just as invasive as their cousins are. I killed it quickly with a knife to the brain. (I consider this to be more humane than the standard decapitation, and it exposes less surface area on the interior to potential bacterial contamination.) It's a testament to the size of these fish that it took me a good five minutes to extract the four-inch hunting knife from the carp's head.

Justin soon had a smaller carp, then Patrick hauled in a mirror carp. At first glance, the mirror carp looks like a different species. It has very few scales, which are widely distributed over its body, as opposed to most other carp, which have plenty of scales close together. In fact, mirror carp are simply a kind of common carp that has been bred by humans for its lack of scales.

Carp don't chase down their food. They are mostly herbivorous, though all species will swallow invertebrates and even smaller fish if they have the opportunity. They'll also take a worm on a hook now and then. Anyone fishing for them should cast the bait and then leave it alone for a while, so I put my ball of oatmeal on its hook and let it settle to the bottom of the river. I rested the rod on a forked stick to wait for a bite. With my hands free, I decided to see what I could catch with a rubber worm and the lighter rod I'd borrowed from Patrick.

This turned out to be a mistake. Hoping for a bass, I hooked what I can only presume was a good-size carp. The light rod strained at the heavy weight, bent almost double, then snapped off. The line broke with it. I stared in disbelief at the dark, blank water for a moment before reaching into my pocket for a twenty-dollar bill, which I handed to Patrick as compensation for his rod.

We took a few more common carp before stopping for the day. Back at Patrick's house, we cleaned the fish. I froze enough to fill the cooler for the trip home to Virginia a few days later.

At home, I smoked some of the carp, and it went nicely on toast for breakfast. There was no foul taste, and for a fish so big, I didn't find it to be at all bony. It tasted as good as any other common whitefish, though a bit blander than the game fish, such as crappie and sunfish, that American fishermen are accustomed to eating.

As for the carp in my parents' pond, the battle continues. In addition to nets, standard tackle, snag hooks, and corn, I've chummed oatmeal balls and anything else that ought to work. The fish dive and disappear as soon as I show up.

Many American anglers think of carp as, well, carp, and fail to recognize the various species. Each has a story behind its introduction and may require a different approach to catching it. Common carp were brought to the United States much earlier than were grass carp. German immigrants were accustomed to eating and fishing for them back home and first released them into the wild in the 1830s. Later that century, there was a series of efforts by the federal government to introduce common carp to American rivers. They were touted as a miracle food that would feed a growing country. Carp do indeed grow very large very quickly and can provide a lot to eat with one catch. But carp never became as popular a food as the government had hoped.

The carp that most recently is loathsome to Americans is an invasive species called the silver carp. This Asian native is notorious for leaping high into the air at the sound of an approaching motorboat. Seeing one fish do this is remarkable. When a hundred are leaping at once, it's downright surreal.

Silver carp were brought to this country, for aquaculture purposes, in the 1970s. At the time, the species was appealing because of its astounding efficiency at converting suspended phytoplankton in the water into fish flesh. It doesn't need to deliberately feed; it's equipped with a unique spongy pad on its gills that soaks up the finest of algal particles from the water as the water passes into the mouth and through the gills. This fish literally eats as it breathes.

Aquaculture researchers looked at this trait and the rapid growth of silver carp as being ideally suited to turn wastewater treatment facilities into centers of food production. The high phosphorus content of the sewage resulted in huge blooms of plankton, which a carp could transform directly and rapidly into protein, growing up to a foot in length in its first year of life.

From the aquaculture perspective, this plan worked extremely well. The fish thrived in the wastewater ponds. There were, however, two problems. First, the FDA didn't even want to discuss the idea of allowing the carp to be sold as food. After all, let's face it, these fish were swimming around in water contaminated with human feces. Who wants to eat the poop fish?

The second problem was that despite the research that private businesses and federal agencies had conducted in advance, the fish escaped into the wild, and did well there, too. Nobody had predicted or even thought this would happen, mostly because silver carp didn't seem to spawn readily outside of their native range. Research had suggested that silver carp wouldn't be a problem if they escaped. One of the funny things about silver carp, though, is that even when they're hardly spawning at all, you still end up with a lot of fish. The fry grow so fast that they quickly reach a size that protects them from most predation. When they're still small, they don't need to stray far from protective cover in order to feed (especially if there's a lot of phytoplankton around for them to take in as they breathe).

Eventually, it became clear that the silver carp in the wastewater treatment ponds were spawning and that the eggs were drifting many miles downstream. The mature fish became established in rivers all over the Midwest, and in some stretches of river, they now constitute up to ninety-five percent of the animal biomass.

The stories I had heard about invasive silver carp sounded too strange to be true, especially the one about their habit of leaping out of the water in response to the sound of a boat's engine. Imagine: enormous silver fish hurtling through the air at speeds fast enough to kill somebody and sometimes jumping into a boat. A refreshing change from conventional fishing, that's for sure.

After watching grainy YouTube videos of these leaping carp, I desperately wanted to see the phenomenon for myself. I also wanted to eat one. Carp in general have a reputation among American fishermen for being inedible, even though most of those fisherman have never actually tried it. I don't dismiss anything that moves as a food source until I've eaten it myself.

Out of the blue, I received an invitation from Jim Low, whom I had met at an outdoor writers conference in Utah. Jim is president of the Outdoor Writers Association of America, and also happens to be the print news coordinator for the Missouri Department of Conservation. Would I like to come out to Missouri for a few days and see these silver carp in action? Would I like to cook up a mess with one of the agency's biologists?

I told Jim I'd be hitting the road as soon as humanly possible.

I didn't even have to pack. By that time, I'd been on the road hunting and fishing for alien species for the better part of a year. The crab traps, fishing rods, guns, camping gear, and spices lived in the car. My suitcase hadn't been emptied in months.

I made the eight-hundred-eighty-eight-mile drive to Columbia, Missouri, in two days. There was a time when I would have tried to do it all in one, but during my adventures in the last year, I had come to enjoy a lot of small things about being on the road. Eating at run-down old barbecue joints and roadside fruit stands. Pulling off to check out a state park, curious after seeing a sign. Picking up a hitchhiker on those rare occasions when there was room for a passenger. You miss out on those things when you try to rack up almost nine hundred miles in a single day. Not to mention that driving as you're falling asleep is a recipe for disaster.

Once I'd gotten out of the familiar mountains and coal country of Virginia and West Virginia, the landscape was new. I crossed a river and went through a big town full of smokestacks and soon found myself in the midst of low, steeply rolling hills covered with grass and dotted with stands of hardwoods. I thought of hills like these as foothills — a prelude to mountains a short distance away. But these hills continued on as far as I could see.

I was into real horse country now and closing in on Lexington, Kentucky. The road cut through blasted-away sedimentary rock with unfamiliar layers of geological stories; I wanted to pull over and climb onto those man-made cliffs and look at the rocks up close and touch them. On an interstate highway, though, that's usually frowned on.

Eventually those low grassy hills gave way to more trees until, suddenly, I became aware of the absence of hills with that keen, eerie sensation that is understood by anyone who grew up surrounded by mountains. The landscape was flat and open to the wide sky above. I was into Indiana, then Illinois. Cornfields lined the road, most of them low and brown with drought. I stopped in a town called Burnt Prairie, looking for lunch and finding only a gas station.

Missouri is a state I still can't quite get a handle on. Sometimes it feels like the Great Plains and other times it seems like the South. Even the accents are all over the map.

I met Jim in the parking lot of a Department of Conservation field station in Columbia. We were quickly joined by biologist Vince Travnichek, who manages the field station. One of Vince's employees, Kevin, drove a pickup truck into the lot with a surprisingly large flat-bottomed boat in tow. We loaded the boat and truck with gear and drove to a tributary of the Missouri River that Vince thought would yield some silver carp.

Vince is a slightly portly man of middle age who seemed quite cheerful for someone who had given up caffeine a few days before. Decades into a career in biology, he still had an obvious enthusiasm for his field, apparent whenever the subject of fish was raised.

We backed the boat down a ramp into the water and the men began setting up a pair of long steel booms off the bow. This was the electrofishing gear — dangling metal tubes like wind chimes that touched the water in order to conduct electricity into it. In fact, the whole boat was designed specifically for electrofishing. Now I was getting very excited; I'd long wanted to see this unusual fishing method in action.

Electrofishing is used by biologists to zap anything within range of the current. This causes the fish to rise to the surface, where they can be observed. Vince assured me that the fish (with one exception) are only stunned and more than ninety-nine percent of the fish he zapped while sampling would soon swim away and go about the rest of their lives with no trouble at all. The one exception is silver carp. For reasons not fully understood, they have a high mortality rate over the few days after being zapped. This was okay by me.

It turns out that electrofishing is not the silver bullet I had thought it was. The current doesn't go very deep, and bottom dwellers usually aren't affected by it. Catfish, in particular, are underrepresented in electrofishing surveys. But this thing was still incredibly cool. Once we were under way, Jim and Vince flipped on the current, and a steady stream of baby shad bubbled up behind the electrofishing booms. I stood with a long-handled net ready to scoop up anything interesting. I handled a longnose gar for the first time. I saw buffalo fish and freshwater drum for the first time.

Suddenly something broke out of the water and landed with a smack about ten feet away. A carp! Then another, then another.

We hadn't been on the water for more than five minutes when I was able to scoop up my first five-pound carp from where it had been stunned by the electricity. The relief at dropping it into the live well was enormous. As of that moment, the trip was a success and I knew I hadn't driven close to nine hundred miles, not counting the return trip, for nothing.

Carp were leaping everywhere. At times there were a dozen in the air at once. Pretty soon we didn't even need the electrofishing gear. Huge carp were jumping straight into the boat without any encouragement from us. It was perhaps the most amazing thing in nature I'd ever witnessed. Big silvery torpedoes of some twenty pounds launched themselves out of the water as high as ten feet in a fast graceful arc right into the middle of the boat. They smacked into the aluminum and flopped around in bloody confusion as I tried to pounce on one, even as another came hurtling in.

It's not often that anything turns out to be exactly as advertised. The silver carp situation in Missouri is one of those few.

As stunning as this was to experience, it's a real problem on many rivers. Think about what happens when a twenty-pound missile of meat and bone hits you in the face. People have already suffered broken bones. One young man went through months of reconstructive surgery after his face was crushed by a particularly large carp. It's only a matter of time before someone is killed; a small child could easily die from one of these hitting the wrong spot. Boaters realize this, and there has been a big reduction in pleasure boating on tributaries of the Missouri. This is not a good thing. When people stop seeing a river, they begin to care less about protecting it.

The oddest part of the story is that silver carp are not known for engaging in this behavior in China. They'll jump now and then, but nothing like what happens in the United States. I'm reminded of the black spiny-tailed iguanas in Florida and their unexpected carnivorousness.

What the leaping silver carp and the rapacious iguanas have in common is that both of these invasive populations descend from a bottleneck population of just a few introductions. One explanation could be that an unusual characteristic — even one that's actually disadvantageous — can become widespread if the other advantages the species has in that new environment are great enough. Such a characteristic, like jumping straight out of the water at the sound of a boat's propeller, might disappear from the gene pool before it was even noticed by humans in the original and more competitive environment. When there are only a few individuals in a new habitat where there are few predators and an advantage in feeding behavior, that oddball trait could persist and eventually become normal.

This was what happened with the silver carp. Jumping out of the water and smashing into things doesn't do them a bit of good. Aside from the boat, I saw carp accidentally flopping themselves out on shore, hitting tree trunks, and getting tangled up in the branches of fallen trees. In some cases, these fish were beating themselves bloody, and nothing useful whatsoever results from this bizarre action. Yet they have such an advantage in feeding behavior over other fish that they still dominate.

As highly efficient filter feeders, they don't have to burn calories swimming in order to eat. Nor do they have to leave a place that feels safe. As long as the current is flowing and has some zooplankton and phytoplankton in it, they don't need to go anywhere. Every time this fish breathes, it eats.

In the space of fifteen minutes we had more than a hundred pounds of fish on board. Even at that, none of the Missourians seemed impressed. They were almost apologetic at the lack of any forty- or fifty-pounders. For my part, the state had more than lived up to its "Show Me" reputation.

Vince pointed out that we had plenty of silver carp and asked what I wanted to do next. What I really wanted to do was grab fish out of the air all day long, but I had a job to finish. We hadn't gotten any common carp or bighead carp, and I wanted to conduct a taste test among the different species.

Bighead carp would be tough, Vince thought. But we'd try.

Bigheads look as if they were put together upside down. Their eyes are absurdly low on their heads. They were brought to the United States for the same reasons silver carp were. They're also filter feeders and have a similar impact on a habitat where they've become common. But they differ from silver carp in two ways.

First, bigheads absorb somewhat larger particles than silver carp do. Silver carp get more food out of every gulp of water in the long run. As a result, there are fewer bigheads in a given stretch of water as silver carp numbers increase (although bigheads colonize a new area first).

Second, bigheads don't jump. Unlike silver carp but like grass carp, they're shy about anything happening above the water's surface. Bigheads and grass carp swim away from approaching boats, humans, and electrical current in the water. This habit makes them difficult to sample with electrofishing gear.

The tactic Kevin and Vince used was to approach piles of brush along the banks and then crank up the current. At first I thought bigheads prefer that type of underwater structure, but I later found out that this ploy works only now and then, because when the bigheads swim away from the boat and into the brush, they get tangled up and can't escape quickly enough from the current before they get a full dose of electricity and float to the surface.

We didn't manage to get any bigheads, but we did stumble upon a nice fat common carp. Bagging two invasive species in one day is always a successful outing, in my opinion. My satisfaction was dampened, though, because aside from the baby shad (usually under three inches in length), the native fish in our electrofishing survey were outnumbered at least fifty to one by invasive carp. This was not a healthy, biodiverse river.

Back at the field station, we filleted the carp and prepared to cook them. Cleaning carp properly is very different from working on most other fish. You carve off the fillets without bothering to gut the fish. Although refrigerated fillets will keep as well as the meat of any other fish, if they're attached to the rest of the fish, they'll quickly spoil. The clock is ticking faster than it is for a largemouth bass or a trout. I later spoke with a commercial carp fisherman and broker who refuses to buy from other fishermen if the carp aren't still alive. Perhaps this is why so many Americans think carp is inedible. If they carry it around on a stringer for too long before eating it, the result won't do much for their appetite.

Vince offered an excellent tip for prepping carp: Unless you like a very fishy-tasting fish, remove and discard the dark red flesh. There isn't much of it, but it's clearly visible on a fillet and you can trim it off easily.

After most of the fish were carved up, Vince heated oil in a pan on a charcoal fire out back. While we waited for the coals to settle down, we were joined by Duane Chapman, research fish biologist for the U.S. Geological Survey. Duane doesn't toot his own horn, but other biologists have assured me that he's the world's top expert on invasive carp.

Duane is a big man, maybe six foot four, with a dark black beard and a ruddy tan from a lot of field hours. We sat at a picnic table and there commenced an hour and a half of the best conversation about fish I've ever had.

Duane's research is pragmatic, and focuses on eradication. Right now he's working on mimicking a chemical mating signal that attracts mature bighead carp to a central location. Because bigheads make such an effort to avoid boats, this lure could make a big difference in scientists' ability to accurately sample populations. It could also make simple work of netting a big heap of the fish in an eradication program.

The first plate of sizzling-hot battered silver carp came out of the oil and onto the picnic table. I blew on a piece to cool it, then popped it into my mouth. It didn't have the outstanding flavor of lionfish; it actually didn't have much flavor at all. It tasted like cod, or like any other firm whitefish. Very few Americans would be able to tell the difference.

Next came a plate of the common carp. The flavor was slightly better in a way that I have difficulty describing. Sweeter, maybe? I liked them both, but the common carp was a tad better than the silver. After trying both species, I figured the concept of carp being inedible had to be the result of people eating fish that had hung around too long before being filleted. There was nothing fishy about either of them.

I LEFT MISSOURI WITH A COOLER FULL OF CARP and my head teeming with thoughts about entire rivers with hundreds of tons of a highly edible fish per mile and almost nobody in America eating them.

Before heading for Virginia, I had one more stop to make. Vince had arranged a meeting for me at an IHOP with a commercial fisherman named Cliff. Like a lot of other watermen today,

Cliff cobbles together a living from a number of little things. He catches sturgeon for part of the year; he and his wife harvest the eggs for caviar, which they ship to buyers around the world, mostly in Russia and Japan. Cliff also fishes for catfish, bigheads, and silver carp.

He uses several types of large nets for different situations and different waters. He rounds up bigheads and catfish by laying out several hundred yards of long net around a dike, where the fish tend to congregate in large numbers. The fish are corralled tighter and tighter until the net can be hauled onto the boat.

Wild-caught catfish are an easy sell to domestic markets. Carp are a little tougher, but Cliff still gets paid. He sells some directly to local grocery stores, where they retail for about two dollars per pound. It's always the least expensive meat in a store. A few years ago, there were very few buyers, but with the recession, folks have gotten less fussy. Large wholesalers are shipping carp fillets to China, where the heads are also popular in soup. In order to be salable, though, the heads must be of very high quality and cut just the right way. Most of what's left is sold for as little as seven cents per pound and turned into fertilizer.

The biggest marketing hurdle in this country is that, as mentioned earlier, consumers don't want to eat carp. If it had any other name, it would probably fly off the shelf (or, really, out of the freezer compartment or the fresh-fish counter). Cliff also mentioned the lack of factories equipped to process huge amounts of carp — a moot point until the public is ready to buy it.

According to Cliff, most of the other guys out there fishing for carp (they're all men) are barely surviving. Many are locked into exclusive contracts with a large buyer that sends the heads to China and grinds the rest into fertilizer. They're getting paid anywhere from seven to fifteen cents per pound, and the buyer sometimes goes months on end without paying them at all. They'd walk away, but there just aren't any other jobs. Their equipment is falling apart and they can barely pay for the gas it takes to get out on the water. There isn't much of an incentive for people to start catching carp in meaningful numbers.

If public demand for the fish causes the wholesale price to go up to twenty-five cents a pound, Cliff thinks that all of this will change. The fishermen will be able to pay their bills again, replace their tattered nets, and hire crews. More people will see it as a business worth getting into. If the public discovered what carp tastes like and came to value it even half as much as cod, the Missouri River system would begin to recover from the carp problem within a few years.

But can people really accept carp as a staple? Back home in Virginia, my wife fried strips of the carp I'd brought home and served them to our children, ages four and seven. They dipped the fish sticks in ketchup and tartar sauce and ate most of what was on their plates. They never bothered to ask what it was.

Nutria

MONTHS AFTER RETURNING from the lizard hunt on Boca Grande, I got an e-mail from Jeff Latham, the journalist I'd met there. We'd kept in touch online since meeting in Florida, and now he wanted to pitch an article about my work with invasive species to a national men's magazine. We went down the list of species and trips that I had coming up, and after a long detour in which we hoped to be running off to Alsace-Lorraine for wild boar, we somehow settled on chasing nutria around the swamps of Louisiana.

In spite of the odd name, nutria is neither an artificial sweetener nor a brand of dog food. Rather, it's a very large semiaquatic rodent from South America. Imagine a beaver with a round tail that breeds as rapidly as a Norwegian rat. Known by some indigenous peoples as *coypu,* the animal was encountered by Spanish explorers who seem to have mistaken it for the otter — thus its name, *nutria,* which is Spanish for otter. The name stuck and followed the animal to North America.

Beginning in the late nineteenth century, nutria were exported around the United States and Europe for use as breeding stock on fur farms. The price of nutria skins was never as high as that of beaver skins, but the animals grew so big so rapidly that they could be raised in captivity much more easily and profitably. A female nutria can be ready to breed at three months old, and she can become pregnant again the day after giving birth.

As fur prices vacillated, fur-ranching operations occasionally went bust, and the remaining nutria were often released into the wild. Populations became established in Louisiana in the 1930s, though it was decades before anyone realized how much of a problem they would become.

Nutria usually live in small family groups in burrows they dig into the banks of bodies of water; this habit leads to heavy erosion.

Riverbanks collapse and levees weaken to the point of failure. And as Hurricane Katrina demonstrated, Louisiana's levee system is extremely important to the survival of its human inhabitants.

Nutria also out-compete the native muskrats, and sometimes beavers, for limited resources. Both nutria and muskrats are herbivores that eat similar foods in the same areas. In the long run, the muskrats lose out where the two species overlap; the nutria breed faster and outnumber the muskrats over time. Also, large groups of nutria will sometimes attack a beaver lodge in force, killing the beavers and taking over the lodge as their own.

They also have a dramatic effect on the native flora. In fact, the damage they inflict on the plants of Louisiana is far out of proportion to their food needs. Inexplicably, nutria will chew through the stalk of a plant in order to eat five percent of it, wasting the other ninety-five percent as they move on to the next one.

With their notoriously high numbers in the drainage canals of New Orleans, I expected nutria to be one of the easier species to bag, and then eat. It seemed like a sure thing to bring Jeff along to get what he needed for his article.

There was just one hitch: The editor of the men's magazine wanted the article to be set in the swamps and bayous rather than in urban New Orleans. My plan had been to follow members of the Jefferson Parish SWAT team for a few nights while they shot nutria from the backs of pickup trucks. Apparently, this didn't seem atmospheric enough for the magazine (although it sounded like a hoot to me).

So I started looking into where else I could hunt nutria. There happens to be a season of sorts for hunting them. On public land, certain months are designated for shooting and trapping the rodents, and even then there are bag limits. This seems like a strange set of rules for hunting a species that the state of Louisiana considers public enemy number one.

My trip would not be occurring anywhere near the start of the regular season, meaning I could hunt either on a government cull trip (already nixed by the magazine) or on privately owned land. On private land in Louisiana, any landowner can kill (or assign someone else to kill) nutria if the animals are causing any type of damage. Because damage goes along almost automatically with the presence of nutria outside their native range, it's pretty much open season on nutria on private land year-round.

For a solid month I begged everyone I knew or met or bumped into at the grocery store for introductions to anyone who owned some land anywhere in Louisiana that had nutria on it. Eventually my begging paid off with an introduction to someone with family property outside Shreveport, in the northwest corner of the state. I even found a local professional trapper, one Michael Beran, who was willing to show us the ropes.

Jeff and I began making preparations for the Great Nutria Expedition of 2011. Jeff had never fired a gun, but had hopes of hunting nutria himself on this trip. To this end, I offered to give him a crash course in safe hunting. We put together a plan for me to pick him up at the train station in Charlottesville, Virginia, teach him basic riflery before dark, and then start the two-day drive to Shreveport in the morning.

I figured that within a couple of days, we'd bag some nutria meat to cook, drive to New Orleans to cook it with a respected chef there, and then go bar-hopping at jazz clubs for the rest of the week until Jeff's flight home. I'd drive back to Virginia at my own pace and there we'd be. Then, a little over a week before leaving, I got the word that the magazine would be sending a photographer along with us. He would fly into Shreveport to meet up with Jeff and me, and we'd go off hunting the next day.

Now, photography is a wonderful thing. I'm all in favor of it. My experiences in bringing photographers along on hunting expeditions, however, have been mixed at best. The difficulty lies in competing interests. My job as the hunter is to avoid detection by my prey for as long as necessary in order to find and kill it. The photographer's job is to take pictures, which often involves noisily moving into positions that make for great angles but spook the prey or block shots. This situation doesn't always work out well.

For two days, Jeff and I had a fine drive across the South in a car full of guns and ammunition. I pulled off at no-name diners in order to acquaint Jeff's English palate with the finer points of regional barbecue. (By the way, the more run-down and sketchy a southern barbecue joint looks, the better the food will be. You can take that to the bank.) We discovered a common love of ABBA and Adam Ant, and blasted them all across Mississippi. One can be very secure in one's masculinity when one is armed to the teeth.

Shreveport surprised me by its strong resemblance to Reno, Nevada. I'm not sure what I was expecting on my first visit to Louisiana, but a casino on every block wasn't it. We met up with our photographer, Red, and checked into our hotel.

The next morning, we bought our hunting licenses and set out to find our hunting ground. I was stunned at the price of a nonresident hunting and fishing license — thirty dollars a day to hunt small game and another five dollars to fish. I swallowed hard and dropped more than a hundred dollars for the privilege of hunting giant rats for the next three days (with a little fishing on the side).

It was a thirty-minute drive out of the city to where we'd be staying on Caddo Lake, which straddles the northwest border between Texas and Louisiana and is home to alligators, gar, largemouth bass, snapping turtles, catfish, cottonmouths, and wading birds of all sorts. Our host, Jarrett Carter, has a spare cottage built beside his family's main home only about a hundred yards from the lake. He graciously allowed us to sack out in his cottage for as long as we needed to find and shoot some nutria.

Michael, my professional trapper contact, pulled up in front of the cottage in his truck full of traps, and we walked along the shore discussing the finer points of nutria hunting. He used traps for most of the nutria hunting he did for clients, but he thought shooting would work, too. He was pretty sure they'd float after being shot in the water. He also confirmed my hunch about some nutria tracks I'd seen along the shore, and pointed out some other signs that I'd missed: for example, a small mound of soil and vegetation near the water with tracks around it. Nutria construct these mounds and sit on them at night. It's not clear why they do this; some trappers believe the nutes are using the mounds for scent marking, to communicate with other nutria. They also seem to prefer to feed while standing on top of them. On later hunts I usually found one of these mounds wherever there were other signs of heavy nutria traffic.

Deep scrapes in the grass were the result of nutria feeding on the lawn, Michael thought. We found marks on the sides of cypress trees where they had clawed off strips of bark. Once I was tuned in to them, I saw signs of nutria everywhere.

As sunset approached, Michael left me with the very valuable loan of a pair of high-tech flashlights. Each light emits a special green laser beam that nocturnal animals don't seem to react to.

These handheld lasers would enable us to illuminate our prey long enough to get off a shot.

The three of us were feeling pretty good as the sun went down. We sat on the comfortable porch looking out to the water. Every few minutes, someone would scan the shoreline with the laser while Jeff or I held a rifle ready to shoot. This seemed like a grand way of hunting nutria. New Orleans was as good as ours. Jeff and Red had the air of men who had struck out on a great adventure, and I couldn't blame them.

Yet the critters never chose to appear. After a night of unsuccessful hunting punctuated by flashbulbs from Red's camera, we packed it in at three in the morning. Waking up in the full heat of a Louisiana summer, we spent part of the afternoon fishing to kill time until dusk, at which time I started asking everyone in sight about hunting nutria. The neighbor helping to stain the deck on Jarrett's parents' house had a hot tip on where to find some nutria for sure. He gave us directions to a drainage canal in a backwater area of the swamp a few miles away, on pipeline land owned by Citgo. He assured me that nobody would care about some nutria hunting.

At this point, I should clarify what the reality is regarding the limits on nutria hunting in Louisiana. In theory, as I said, there's a season and bag limits on anything but private land with verified damage. In *practice*, though, people just want the nutria gone and they welcome any effort to clear them out. I spoke with professional nuisance-wildlife trappers in several parishes, local hunters, game wardens, and at least one sheriff's deputy and the opinion was universal. As long as you aren't in someone's backyard, in a park, or in a wildlife management area out of season, nobody cares. They just want the nutria dead.

The official regulatory view of nutria in Louisiana is oddly conflicted, a result of opinions changing over time. When it first showed up in the wild, the nutria was seen as a beneficial natural resource. Trappers in the 1950s had it designated as a fur-bearer, which automatically qualified it for inclusion in all sorts of rules and restrictions designed to allow a fur-bearing species to be hunted in a limited way that ensures its continued presence.

Over the next few decades, it started to become clear that nutria were going to be an ecological disaster. The Army Corps of Engineers found levees riddled with holes and burrows that made them vulnerable to collapse after flooding. Conservationists noticed nutria's negative effect on native wildlife. Even though the value of nutria pelts was steadily dropping (on a good day, they now go for around five dollars apiece), the old-time trappers didn't want them to stop being regulated as fur-bearers.

The result was a mixed bag of regulations. On the one hand, Louisiana offers a bounty program for nutria killed by hunters registered through its program. The state also allows the animals to be killed without limit on private land. On the other hand, on public land and waterways there are official bag limits and seasons that were designed to ensure that the species could recover from the hunting of the previous season.

What I found happening in real life is that the fur-bearer status is being ignored by both hunters and law-enforcement agents in most areas. Although one hopes to see sensible laws that are followed and enforced with consistency, Louisiana has a political process that is notorious for corruption, and perhaps what goes on is the best that can be hoped for.

We drove to the canal to see whether the backwater area Jarrett's neighbor had mentioned was accessible by boat. After spending a long time hunting the bank of that canal by the road and catching a glimpse of at least one nutria, we decided to come back after dark. By boat.

Jarrett's flat-bottomed jon boat wasn't very big. It could hold two people comfortably and had accommodated three of us with fishing rods only with careful arrangement and balancing of bodies. After rounding up a fresh battery, we'd be able to use the trolling motor, which would be essential for the three miles of water we had to cross to reach the swampy backwater intended as our hunting ground. But that also meant a lot more weight.

We needed Jarrett on board to navigate us to and from the swamp. Lake Caddo covers more than twenty-four thousand acres and has numerous inlets, swamps, and creeks in which to get helplessly lost. Although man-made, it's big enough and wild enough to be considered a serious candidate for Sasquatch habitat. Hundreds of Bigfoot sightings have been reported around Lake Caddo, according to the Texas Bigfoot Research Conservancy.

Considering the total weight and bulk of people and gear, I suggested we leave Red, the photographer, behind. That idea was not well received by Red, so we all piled into the boat, which was already filled with guns, gear, battery, and motor. We had barely three inches of freeboard between the surface of the water and the top of the boat. One good wave from a passing power boat and we could be in real trouble.

A warm breeze picked up as we quietly motored out into the middle of the lake. I sat in the bow with my shotgun, one of Michael's magic green lasers, and a flashlight. Still far from where we could hope to spot any nutria, I flipped on the flashlight and pointed it into the water. Fish and turtles were illuminated, often only inches from my light.

Long, pale gar of two and three feet long slipped past me like reptilian ghosts. A carp looked startled and bumped into the front of the boat as it fled.

Behind me, Jeff and Jarrett chatted about guitars. Every now and then, the motor would sputter out for no apparent reason and Jarrett would fiddle with it until it got going again.

Sometimes we found ourselves within patches of giant salvinia, an invasive aquatic plant that floats on the surface in clumps. Native to Brazil, it, like so many other invasive species, is thought to have ended up in the wild after it was imported for use as an ornamental plant in aquariums and ponds. The stuff forms patches that each cover several acres on Lake Caddo; when we found ourselves entering one, we had to shut off the motor to avoid fouling the propeller. There was nothing to do except paddle manually through it. We left the open water and moved among a number of cypress trees growing up from the water. A dilapidated duck blind was built around one of them, and this marked the rough boundary of the swamp where the nutria might be found.

By this time, I was figuring out some of the behavioral patterns of the nutria on this lake. Open grassy areas like the one behind Jarrett's cottage provide good feeding grounds but aren't a suitable place for nutria to live. The gentle slope of the shore doesn't provide much of an embankment to burrow into; therefore, the nutria were making a pretty long commute to feed on people's lawns. It seemed likely that they were maintaining burrows on the steep sides of creeks and drainage canals that feed into the lake. The tracks in the mud behind Jarrett's house were of different sizes and had been made on different days, suggesting the nutria made regular visits.

This means there were three types of places to ambush nutria: where they live, where they eat, and along the path between those places. The theory wasn't all that different from what I'd experienced hunting whitetail deer or any other animal with predictable habits in a well-defined territory.

It would be easy to miss commuting nutria swimming across the open water, but in the closer confines of the swamps and creeks, there was less water to watch and it would be easier to spot nutria on the move. This was why we were steering the boat into the swamp.

Now considering the hunt to be on, I loaded my shotgun but kept the safety switch engaged. I had chosen the shotgun because I would probably be shooting at a moving target from a moving boat. Shotguns throw out a cloud of pellets that make it easier to intercept a moving object than it would be with, say, a single bullet from a rifle. I also carried a loaded revolver on my hip for the remote but real possibility of an alligator attack.

I turned to say something to Jeff when suddenly a flash went off from the photographer's camera. It blinded me, and for the next few minutes I saw nothing but floating balls of light. This happened several times during the boat ride.

We slipped past a snake coiled around the branch of a cypress tree and heard a bird hooting from far away. The water grew more and more shallow. We were now in honest-to-goodness swamp with a cacophony of insects and frogs. There were little clicking sounds and cicada-like whirring and the deep honking of bullfrogs. I had seen swamps in the daytime, but never anything like this, with the promise of alligators and hundred-pound snapping turtles — maybe even Bigfoot himself. Nutria aside, I'd have been happy to spend the rest of the night just sitting there and listening to wildlife going about their business in the swamp.

Something the size and shape of a grown nutria slipped into the water from a hillock of grass. I had the gun up to my shoulder in time but was unable to identify the species with enough certainty to take a shot.

The weeds became too thick for the propeller, so we paddled and poled our way forward. (At several key spots, the butt of my shotgun made an excellent bargepole.) Finally, we were well and truly grounded. At the mouth of the system of canals and creeks where we knew there were nutria, we could go no farther on account of how low the flat-bottomed boat sat in the water. There were simply too many people with too much weight. Thus, we turned around and went back to the cottage.

After a few hours of sleep, I sat on the porch and considered the situation. Time was slipping away. We'd seen nutria from the road and knew they were in there. We had to get serious and go in there any way we could.

We drove to the spot where Jarrett had pointed out the nutria the day before and started scouting on foot. I found a number of burrow systems of various ages in the canal along the road and realized that I'd found where they live. I hiked farther into the swamp and discovered an old beaver lodge that appeared to have been taken over by nutria. Lots of nutria tracks, a vegetative mound by the water, and years-old telltale beaver chewing signs on the trees.

I decided to set up an ambush from a dozen yards across the creek from the vegetative mound. If we sat there long enough, eventually a nutria would haul itself out of the water and make its way to the mound. This marked the beginning of a kind of hunting that I'm accustomed to for deer, but it didn't appeal to my journalist friends.

Hunting from a boat is a great adventure. Stalking the shoreline on foot in the dark with a rifle in hand speaks to the Tom

Sawyer hidden within each of us. Sitting still from a concealed position in the swamp for hours on end in silence is an exercise that most people would find excruciating.

Hunting deer, however, had prepared me well for this. I've spent many a day alone, waiting in ambush from dawn to dusk. If you do this enough times, eventually one of two things happens: Either you go home and turn on the TV and swear off hunting altogether or you learn to cross into the Zen of hunting. Your mind enters an altered state of hyperawareness, and boredom is simply not an issue. Time ceases to have any meaning; you really can't tell the difference between fifteen minutes and an hour.

I can't tell you for sure how many days we hunted that swamp. A strange odyssey began during which I rarely slept more than four hours in any day or night. I became an almost wholly nocturnal creature.

During the afternoon, we patrolled on foot from the road. The nutria usually woke up around then and would sit near their burrows feeding, grooming, or sunning themselves. For these excursions, I carried my Ruger target pistol in its holster on my belt. Several times I managed to get off a shot or two before the nutria spooked into the water. Sometimes I was convinced that I'd hit an animal, yet nothing floated to the surface, as Michael said it should. I contemplated wading into the water to search, but the alligator situation coupled with my lack of health insurance discouraged that folly.

One night, an hour after dusk, as Jeff was scanning with a green laser flashlight and I held the shotgun, I saw what was definitely a nutria swimming from the burrow toward the open lake.

"Jeff, move the light on him," I whispered.

The nutria swam past the unmoving beam of light, apparently oblivious.

"Jeff, move the light so I can take the shot!"

The light remained fixed, and the nutria was gone. I turned to Jeff to ask what the hell he was doing and saw that he had a finger in each ear, well protected against both the expected blast of the shotgun and every word I had said.

Most of our hunts were flubbed by this sort of thing. Red would pop a flashbulb or Jeff would start talking loudly. I worked out a technique for holding and aiming the flashlight with my left hand, which also held the fore end of the shotgun.

Despite my growing frustration with them, and our joint disappointment at not getting our nutria, we agreed to have another go. We would spend another day or so hunting, then plan B would be to drive farther south, to Baton Rouge or someplace else where the populations of nutria are denser. The tough thing about plan B was that we didn't know anyone or any place to hunt anywhere other than where we were now.

All of the pieces were there for us to bag some nutria: I had the boat and the gear, and I had those rodents patterned. What I needed were hours of ambush at night without interruption.

That night, as the sun went down, a parade of swamp wildlife began to emerge. Something small and furry sat by the water's edge for a moment before slipping under the surface. A pair of raccoons, large and small, crept along the bank. They didn't react in the slightest to the beam of green light aimed at them. Another lone raccoon appeared later and stopped to grab a crayfish from the edge of the water. An owl flew from tree to tree and hooted.

Some sort of animal came swimming toward me, only its head exposed, with a broad V of wake behind it. I shouldered my gun and began to swing on it before realizing that this was almost certainly a mink. I lowered the gun and watched it disappear.

I had a nutria dead to rights from ambush that night. It was swimming and was within a dozen yards of me when I squeezed the trigger. My left hand couldn't steady the shotgun well, because it was also holding the flashlight; as a result, the shotgun leapt up vertically in my hands. A geyser of water erupted, and when I came out of the flash and recoil, there were only ripples on the surface.

We waited for the nutria to float up in the murky water, but it never did. I searched up and down the creek and found no evidence of it. As I walked back to where Jeff and Red were waiting for me, however, I saw through the woods some dark shape that was roughly man-height. It immediately ran off into the swamp. A black bear? A shy human? Bigfoot? I'll never know. . . .

Dawn found us back at the shore behind the cottage, waiting for feeding activity at first light. Nothing appeared. I was very tired and spirits were low all around, but I was still happy about having had a night in the swamp, observing the nocturnal goings-on. It was strange: The longer we spent out there, the more frustrated I became, yet the more I appreciated sitting in that swamp and the more I looked forward to seeing what tomorrow night would bring.

The next day we were online, madly searching for trappers or nuisance-wildlife specialists who could help us find a nutria at the last minute. I left messages for several people. Meanwhile, I was able to get hold of a French chef who specialized in cooking nutria. Based in Baton Rouge, Philippe Parola could talk to us intelligently about nutria and thought he might be able to find one in the freezer for us to taste.

At least it was something. I reluctantly left the amazing laser flashlights with Jarrett to return to Michael and started the long drive to Baton Rouge.

Listening to Philippe was like trying to drink from a fire hose. He has enormous knowledge and experience with nutria and carp as food. Every sentence he spoke raised a dozen more questions, which would have to wait because the next sentence would be just as fascinating.

Philippe was born and raised in Paris. He began cooking professionally when he was quite young, working at an upscale hotel in London for a while and later serving a few years in the army in Africa. His time as a soldier in the bush got him into the habit of hunting and eating things that most Westerners would not consider food.

Well into middle age now, Philippe has tightly cropped hair and speaks English with an interesting blend of Parisian and Louisianan accents. He has owned a string of successful restaurants but is moving into a new arena of the food business: wholesale processing of invasive species as food. He immediately had my undivided attention.

Several years ago, Philippe decided to do something about the nutria problem in Louisiana. He quickly discovered two important truths about marketing nutria meat. First: The Chinese will consider eating anything. Second: The world at large, including China, is not going to buy or eat nutria meat so long as it sees Louisiana natives turning up their noses at it.

In order to create an export market for the meat, Philippe needed to make the stuff into bona fide local cuisine. He had a good place to start — Cajuns are almost as open-minded in their approach to meat as the Chinese are. He made the rounds of state fairs and food expos, any event where he could cook nutria using his substantial gifts as a chef and then hand out samples. He was interviewed on television and even convinced the governor to publicly try it.

Soon Philippe had grocery stores asking to stock the stuff and restaurants putting it on the menus. His next task was to ensure an adequate wholesale supply of high-quality meat. That meant going out on the bayous and meeting with nutria hunters to teach them new ways to handle the meat. Hunting for the bounty and the hide doesn't require keeping the meat especially fresh. In fact, the way the animal is skinned depends on whether you want a first-class hide or first-class meat.

The hunters learned to process the meat and get it cooled quickly. Working all day long from airboats, they were able to harvest thousands of the invasive rodents daily.

Soon Philippe had a pretty good business going across Louisiana. The state began to embrace the meat as its own cuisine, and sales were good. Not good enough to support the back end of the business, but there was definitely a demand.

It was time to take the next step, overseas. Philippe traveled to Japan, Taiwan, several countries in Europe, and China with samples of nutria. He had sales figures and media clippings to show that this was something Americans ate. Wholesalers soon were hooked, and Philippe had his first orders for refrigerated shipping containers full of nutria meat. This would command a price per nutria much higher than that for the furs and bounty, creating an economic incentive for local hunters to clear out the species without government programs or spending.

Orders in hand, Philippe began the process of paperwork for the lawful export of his shipping containers. That's when he hit an important roadblock: from the Food and Drug Administration.

The FDA is one of the agencies that regulate not only the interstate commerce of food but also its export. The agency has a rule regarding sales of meat other than fish: It must be killed in an FDA-approved slaughterhouse. If wild nutria could be rounded up alive in significant numbers, this might be a possibility. Unfortunately, though, they can't. They must be killed in the field and processed later.

On this point, the FDA refused to budge or even discuss the matter. With this blow, Philippe's brilliant scheme to rid Louisiana of nutria fell apart.

The odd thing was that there were no complaints about food safety from any of the export destinations. The FDA was not protecting American consumers or enforcing any international trade agreement; indeed, the wild harvest of meat is legal and ordinary in much of the rest of the world. Culled antelope from Africa winds up on European market shelves and menus. Wild boar and red deer in Germany, France, and the United Kingdom are quickly transported to butchers after being shot in the wild, and the meat is sold commercially. No disasters or health crises abroad have resulted from this system. Foreign markets are happy to accept wild-harvested invasive meat from the United States, but our own government is blocking the sale.

IT WAS GETTING LATE, and we wanted to drive to the village of Port Vincent to meet a trapper who thought he could hook me up with some nutria. Philippe offered to come along, so I left my car in the parking lot and rode with him to the village, about half an hour outside of Baton Rouge. Red and Jeff followed.

Port Vincent, Philippe assured me in his odd Parisian twang, was as pure and true an example of southern Louisiana in spirit and appearance as one could hope for. Population seven hundred and forty one, as of the 2010 census.

We met trapper Carter Lambert in front of his house. He was in his late twenties or early thirties. After introductions, I asked him if he would show me his hands. Confused, he held them out, palms down. Sure enough, they were covered with the telltale scars of an experienced wildlife professional. I figured this guy knew what he was doing.

A few hundred yards behind Carter's house is a creek that feeds into the nearby Amite River. We were burning daylight, so we decided to get straight to the hunting. Carter drew a battered old Marlin Model 60 .22 rifle from the back of his pickup truck. It looked older than either of us.

"Family gun?" I asked him.

"Yup."

Yeah. Carter definitely knew what he was doing.

THE TERRAIN AND FLORA of Port Vincent were noticeably different from what we'd left behind, near Shreveport, that morning. The northern part of the state has more conifers and less overall brush. This place was a jungle. Darwin's "tangled bank" was never more vivid to me than in the slow-motion war going on among the denizens along that creek.

The pale torpedo outline of a moderate gar greeted me at the water's edge. Along the banks, I saw nutria burrow systems of various ages. The older ones were abandoned and exposed along their length by the erosion they had created, and in many places the bank was collapsing. I reflexively held my scoped .22 rifle in front of my face (with the barrel pointed at the sky) to break the substantial spiderwebs in front of me. There was no trail; we simply followed the creek. Thorns scraped my arms.

Carter stopped us by the water for a moment.

"Now look, y'all," he said. "This is a little different from where y'all just came from. Every step you take, you have to be looking for snakes. We got cottonmouths everywhere this close to the water. When you're along the bank like this, you don't get close without looking for gators. You see something like a log close by, back up. You see little bubbles near the shore, back up."

"Yeah, we know," I said. "We just spent a week hunting around Lake Caddo." I felt like an old pro in gator country by now.

"That's nothing like here. The gators are a lot bigger and there's a lot more of them."

Carter was right. The area was crawling with alligators, cottonmouths, wild boars, critters of every persuasion.

We set up with our rifles across the creek (which was about forty feet wide and of unknown depth) from what were obviously active burrows. Carter explained that active burrows are always cleared of any leaves or debris in front of the entry. I watched the opposite bank while Carter told Jeff stories of his time in the Louisiana National Guard during Hurricane Katrina as one of only two medics assigned to guard and care for an entire hospital.

A light rain began to fall and the sun was failing us. My scope fogged up. Fortunately, most of my hunting rifles have a scope with quick-detaching rings that enable me to pull it off swiftly in this kind of situation and switch to using the open sights. The chorus of bullfrogs and insects increased to the usual dusk fever pitch. Carter and I realized we would need spotlights in order to continue hunting.

Philippe left to see about a restaurant where we could cook the anticipated kill, and Jeff and Red drove to the store to find spotlights.

Carter had an idea for a new place to hunt while we waited for the others to return. He drove us down a dirt road and pulled onto the shoulder. Somewhere in the dense forest was a lake with an island in the middle. Nutria had burrows on the island and sometimes could be sniped from the shore. The forest was still dripping from the rain. There wasn't any trail, but we forged ahead.

I have to confess to taking a perverse pleasure in this kind of expedition. I enjoy bushwhacking at night through rough country. I did it for weeks on end during an Outward Bound course in the Smoky Mountains and eventually became perfectly comfortable with it. If I had water, the means to make a fire, and a knife, there wasn't much that I needed to worry about. I had all of these items and more as we pushed off into the night.

It was a joy to be in Carter's company as we became really and truly motherless lost in the wilderness. Not only did he have the same appreciation for wandering around in the dark woods as I do, but he was equally unconcerned about our disorientation.

We stumbled across the shore of some body of water and saw many pairs of eyes reflected in the narrow beams of our lights. Alligators of various sizes drifted toward us.

I don't encourage unfounded fears of alligators. Attacks on humans are rare. Jogging on a path around a pond during the day is usually the most risk taken by people who live near alligators. What we were doing in Louisiana was much, much more dangerous.

During this trip, it had dawned on me that I was usually sitting on the edge of the water, within easy lunging distance of an alligator. It was also usually dark, when it's tough to spot a big gator. Then what happens when a nutria is actually shot? Odds are that it slides into the water. Even if it's on the bank, the scent of blood is right there, luring gators to the very spot to which you, the hunter, are making a beeline in order to retrieve your kill.

I decided to take some extra precautions, including making regular sweeps of the water with a light to check for signs of gators, such as rising bubbles and anything that looked like a drifting log. I was glad to have the others with me: People watching out for gators while you're looking for nutria seemed like a good idea. (It's also helpful to have someone to call 911 for you, should an alligator circumvent your vigilance.) Even with a gun at hand, the best defense against alligators is to spot them, then get the hell away before it's too late.

All this was going through my mind as we wandered through the dripping, humid forest — which, I noticed, was permeated by a strange, pungent smell. I asked Carter what it was.

"Cottonmouths. They make that scent when they get mad or you get too close to them."

Good to know.

Eventually, we figured that we had a river within a few miles on one side, a highway on another, and the back road where the truck was waiting on another. If we walked far enough, we could get our bearings. We might end up walking till dawn, but it would work. We made a straight course for the moon to avoid going in circles, and before too long we came out onto the road within a quarter of a mile of the truck. This was dumb luck; we could just as easily have spent the rest of the night out there.

We met up with Jeff and Red in front of Carter's house. They had a couple of spotlights, and I felt good about the chances of our getting some nutria. The burrows were there and active, and we had all night to hunt. And as a last-ditch effort, Carter had some traps to set over the holes; there would surely be a dead nutria in one of them by morning.

Unfortunately, he couldn't go back out to the creek with us, but he gave us permission to hunt his sizable piece of land and offered to show us how to set the traps.

Now, I'm a hunter, not a trapper (rats and mice aside). I had never used one of these things and, frankly, they scared the bejeezus out of me. They scare me even more now that I've seen one in action.

Carter's traps are big iron squares that are placed over the entrances to holes. They snap shut with five hundred pounds of pressure. One false move while you're setting the trap, and your forearm is crushed. He demonstrated how to set one and I recorded it on video for reference in the field.

We had spotlights, traps, a rifle, a creek full of nutria, and the rest of the night. Red and Jeff had to fly home the next day, but the makings of a successful hunt were all there. We said goodnight to Carter and walked to where the road crossed the creek and where we would begin bushwhacking to the ambush we'd sat in earlier.

I turned to Jeff and Carter.

"Okay, guys, we can do this. Jeff, you carry the backpack with the extra gear and water, and hold the trap before I arm it. Red, you hold one of the spotlights and be on gator duty. Sweep the river along us every few steps and tell me if we're approaching a big one. I'll walk point with the rifle, watching for cottonmouths and ready to take a shot at any nutria we see on the way."

Jeff stared at me as if I was crazy.

"There are snakes out there. *Cottonmouths.* Look what I'm wearing! I'm wearing these low-cut shoes."

"Well, I've only got on low-cut hiking boots myself," I said. "And look, if one of us gets bitten by a snake, it's not the end of the world. We're not gonna die. We'll each have two people as backup for first aid and to get an ambulance. It'd be a few nights in a hospital, a week or two of feeling sick, and then a great story for the rest of your life."

They weren't buying it.

“Carter said there are big gators back there,” Red said flatly.

“That’s why we need a dedicated set of eyes on gator patrol. We’ll watch each other’s back.”

I started to walk into the woods, then turned and saw that neither of them had moved. I picked up the heavy iron trap, holding it awkwardly with the same hand that held the flashlight. My rifle was in the other hand. The camouflage backpack full of first-aid supplies and tools remained at Jeff’s feet on the glistening wet asphalt.

I stepped into the woods on my own.

It was a long, slow trip along the tangled bank. Attempting to watch my own back for alligators while scanning for snakes (which were numerous) was awkward, made more so by the burden of the large, heavy iron trap and my rifle. (The shotgun would have been better, but that was sitting in the trunk of my car, many miles away in the parking lot of the restaurant where we’d met up with Philippe.)

At last I reached an active burrow we’d noticed earlier. My mission was to set the trap, leave in one piece, and then come back in the morning. I replayed the video of Carter’s demonstration on my handheld recorder and, copying his actions, set the trap.

My cell phone didn’t have a signal, and it became painfully obvious that if I managed to snap my hand in this trap, there would be no cavalry to the rescue; Jeff and Red were too far away to hear me shout.

Lacking my pack and tools, I used a pocketknife to cut stakes to secure a trap. I noticed a six-foot alligator watching me from a few yards away. I backed up farther onto the bank to finish shaping the stakes.

Without my hatchet, when it came to pounding them into the ground, I used the butt of my poor rifle as a hammer. At this point, the alligator was not to be seen, which was at first a relief but on reflection was more troubling than when I knew where it was.

A snake of indeterminate species watched from the edge of the water as I set the triggers of the trap as best I could. My work done, I withdrew back to the road.

It was a long ride, in the backseat of Red's car, to where I'd parked my car, back in Baton Rouge. Probably longer for him than it was for me.

"You know," I said, breaking the silence, "if the only thing you want out of hunting is killing something, you're bound to be disappointed."

Men often get wrapped up in machismo and questions of identity on their first serious hunts. They go out into the wilderness with ideas about who they are and what they hope to become by virtue of their deeds. What they find out about themselves along the way cannot help but either buoy or break them afterward.

THE TRAP WAS EMPTY IN THE MORNING, probably because of my inexpert setting of the triggers. Jeff and Red were soon on their way to the airport, while I was driving to a diner in Port Vincent to meet Philippe for breakfast.

I walked into Fred's Restaurant and sat down at a table across from Philippe, who was already halfway through his meal with some friends. He introduced me to them, including David Roshto, the owner of Fred's.

David is a wiry, serious-looking man in his mid-fifties with a dry sense of humor. Philippe explained what I was doing in town and I related the story so far. David invited me to stay as long as I wanted to in the basement apartment of his house on the Amite River, only a moment's walk away. Philippe was sure any number of people could get us onto some nutria.

It took a lot of cups of coffee to get myself up to speed after the night I'd had. After breakfast, I brought my bags and gear to David's place. I could hardly believe my luck. After less than twenty-four hours in a new place, I had somewhere to stay, introductions to hunters, a dock to fish from. Most important, I had a place to do the laundry accumulated from a week of haunting swamps.

I took a nap, then returned to Fred's for a catfish po'boy and a beer. A few of the waitresses and customers offered nutria pointers; all suggested I go out on the swamp in an airboat and ride around until I saw some.

Meanwhile, David and Philippe were asking around on my behalf. That afternoon, we made our way to a boat landing. There we met up with a bunch of their Cajun friends, who had brought a trio of airboats they'd built themselves.

An airboat is basically a flat-bottomed hull with a huge fan on the back of it (powered by the biggest engine the boatbuilder can find — usually something on the order of a snowmobile engine, but sometimes as big as the engine of a small airplane). It doesn't have any brakes or a reverse gear. Unlike a conventional powerboat, it has no propeller to become tangled up in weeds. Airboats can even move around on dry land when they need to. The ecological footprint is extremely small; unlike with a prop-driven boat, there's no risk of slicing the back of a manatee.

Every boat is a little bit different, depending on what it will be used for and because each is hand-crafted. The boat I rode in was built to be a work platform along remote oil pipelines through the swamps and bayous, so it was relatively wide, flush-decked, and less maneuverable in tight quarters than would be a boat built for hunting.

A small alligator watched us from the water as David, Philippe, and I each stepped aboard a different airboat with our respective pilots. I rode with Daniel Cupp at the helm. Daniel was born and raised here and has been driving airboats around this very swamp for more than three decades.

The roar of an airplane engine a few feet behind us, separated from us by only a wire cage, made conversation difficult. We pushed along a broad channel, quickly gathering speed. Snowy white ibises and blue-gray herons took to the air as we approached.

Daniel steered us into a narrow channel, where we entered a maze of cypress. The surface of the water was like an undulating lawn covered with algae, duckweed, and grasses that grew from the slightest clump of floating debris. Water hyacinths, occasionally in bloom, bobbed along. Brought from South America by aquaculture hobbyists, water hyacinth has taken over large stretches of water in Louisiana and is perhaps the worst invasive aquatic plant in the country. It impedes water flow, creates ideal microhabitat for mosquitoes, and blocks light from reaching native plants under the surface. Low oxygen levels result, killing fish where the plant is particularly dense.

We slowed as we approached a low-slung cabin with a tattered Confederate flag flying from the gabled roof. We'd arrived at an island hidden in the middle of a vast swamp. Each boat rode onto the shore and parked on dry land.

"This is our deer camp," Daniel announced cheerfully in his Cajun drawl as he shut off the engine.

"Not for long, it ain't," said Dave.

Dave piloted Philippe's boat. He is short and pot-bellied, sports long hair, and is usually good-humored.

"They takin' it. They takin' all of it from us." He spat on the ground in disgust.

The story I gradually got from the usually laconic Dave was that his family had been part of a group that leased the land for hunting going back a century. They hunted alligators and the unique local subspecies of whitetail deer known as blue deer, for the unusual tint of their coat in just the right light. Whoever owned the land on paper had sold it to a federal agency — Dave wasn't sure which and didn't much care — about a year ago.

The group had been told to leave, but none of the guys was inclined to obey. I looked around at the inside of the cabin and saw an array of bunks, like in an army barracks.

"We ain't going," declared Dave. "They gonna have to drag me outta here."

These hunters are armed to the teeth, know the swamp like the back of their hands, and have been there forever. Woe unto to the government employee who finds this place and decides it's a good idea to try to kick them out. Forcibly removing Cajuns from this place would end about as well as Andrew Jackson's crusade against the Seminoles. A lot of fighting and a lot of tears for no good end.

Everybody had a beer except for yours truly, as I was hoping to pull the trigger on a nutria ASAP. For me, it was time to get back on the boats and cruise the swamp, and that's what we did.

Suddenly I became aware of a lot of shouting and gesticulating from one of the other boats. Daniel pointed to a moving brown mass in the water about fifty yards away. A nutria!

I grabbed my .22 rifle (still missing the scope after the previous night) from under the bungee cord that secured it to the deck. I stood up, clicked a loaded magazine into place, and steadied myself as well as I could in a boat that was still moving, although slowly now.

My first shot splashed into the water well behind the nutria. I popped off another and missed again. The third shot struck true and the rodent sank. We pushed in closer to where it had gone down. Philippe's boat arrived first. He leaned over the side, reached underwater, and lifted out a dead nutria.

Huh. I guess sometimes they float and sometimes they sink.

I knocked out another one ten minutes later. I took real satisfaction in lifting the floating carcass by the tail and holding a nutria for the first time, after a long week of hunting them unsuccessfully. The sense of relief was incredible.

Our little squadron set a course for a place called the Dead Zone, where we stopped to break out the beer and dress out the nutria. The Dead Zone is a large open area of shallow water with almost no cypresses or other trees. It covers a few hundred acres and takes its name from the fact that in the height of summer, the water level lowers enough to expose dry land where nothing lives except cottonmouths and the occasional blue deer.

I examined the nutria. Although it was obviously a rodent, it reminded me more of a big rabbit than of the giant rat I'd expected. It was no less appetizing than any other dead thing I've turned into food.

Philippe and Dave each demonstrated their technique for skinning a nutria. Dave's method was tailored more for getting an intact hide, while Philippe's method resulted in more cleanly butchered meat. Philippe insisted that the only parts of the animal worth butchering and keeping were the hindquarters, which form a cut referred to as a saddle. We put the saddles and a hide on ice in the beer cooler and made it back to the boat landing minutes before a thunderstorm hit.

Philippe announced that we'd be taking the saddles back to Fred's to cook them. David Roshto was firmly opposed to this. He didn't want a bunch of swamp rats carried into *his* kitchen. With the easy authority of a celebrated French chef who is accustomed to determining what's what in the kitchen, Philippe assured his old friend that he'd be cooking them there all the same.

"Well, you just take them in through the back door, then. Don't let nobody see you."

Fair enough. We brought in the "swamp rats" through the back door. The staff (Philippe doesn't actually work at Fred's) graciously made room for us on this busy night.

Dressing the saddle wasn't much different from trimming any other meat. The membrane over the muscle is carved away along with any fat (there isn't much on the typical nutria). What was left looked like a perfectly appetizing piece of meat. The color of the smaller nutria was a pale pink. The larger one was a deeper red. Nutria at this stage of the process can be a substitute in most recipes calling for chicken.

Working with the ingredients on hand, Philippe poured Italian salad dressing over both saddles on a baking sheet and then put them in the oven on low heat. As we waited, we moseyed across the parking lot to Fred's On the River, a bar and bait shop that's also owned and run by David Roshto (though founded by his good friend Fred Boyd). Two signs out front caught my eye. One points out the motorcycle-only parking in front; the other reads NO CLUB COLORS. I wondered if I'd be walking into the middle of a biker-gang fight.

Inside the wood-paneled barroom is the most splendid display of local taxidermy imaginable: deer, bobcats, largemouth bass. An eight-foot, full-mount alligator stretched above the liquor bottles with mouth agape. George Strait was banging out from the juke box, bikers played pool with rednecks, and old women danced the two-step with anyone who'd join them. Instantly, I fell in love with the place.

We drank beers at the bar until it was time to check on the nutria. When it was cooked to Philippe's satisfaction, he carved the meat from the bone, shredded it, and seasoned it with a Cajun spice blend (heavy on the ground cayenne pepper and parsley). Then he browned it in a frying pan.

"That doesn't look too bad," David commented as Philippe seasoned the meat. "Kinda like chicken. Smells good, too."

When it was served, over white rice, it looked like, well, normal food. And wonder of wonders, David — the same guy who balked at us carrying the stuff into his restaurant — wanted to try some.

"Hey, Philippe, it's good!" David said, surprise registering in his voice. He took another bite. Then another.

"I can't believe I'm eating nutria."

I took a bite as well. Sure enough, it tasted like chicken. By now, I'd eaten a lot of things that tasted like chicken; every reptile has tasted like chicken. Nutria meat, as Philippe prepared it that night, was indistinguishable from chicken.

We took the rest of the food to the bar and shared it with the bartender and anyone else who was interested. They all thought it was pretty good. Some of the locals had never heard of nutria, though in typical Louisiana style, none of them was afraid to try it.

Philippe left early, but I stayed at Fred's until closing time, two or three in the morning. By that time, half of Port Vincent had offered to take me fishing or hunting. I danced with an elderly woman who'd had both legs amputated below the knees and still managed to tire me out on her prostheses. Maybe I've had a better time on some other night somewhere else, but I sure can't remember it.

The Giant Canada Goose

IT TOOK ME TWO DAYS TO DRIVE HOME from Louisiana. I ruefully drove past New Orleans, by then too low on funds to stop and see the city. I found a New Orleans radio station, WWOZ, that played Cajun music and jazz and kept it on the dial far away to the north, even as it finally crackled with static and gave way to an insipid pop station. I drove across Alabama, Georgia, and Tennessee, through the barbecue belt. When I stopped for the night in a cheap motel, I dreamed of the swamp and the sounds of frogs and cicadas and the taste of cloudy brown swamp water tinged with iodine and cut with lime juice.

How long I had been on the road? I didn't know. I arrived home in the early evening and found an in-box full of e-mail from reporters asking me about geese. Geese? Why geese? Nutria were all that mattered! As I read some more, I discovered that, out of the blue, I had unexpectedly won a long fight with the state of New York over the fate of giant Canada geese.

I DON'T THINK I COULD BRING MYSELF TO HATE or even actively dislike any species of animal — except leeches, mosquitoes, and yellow jackets. (Okay, and ticks.) I've never shared the suburban antipathy toward Canada geese, which suburbanites themselves have usually displaced. You'll hear a lot of complaints about deer and raccoons, too.

My beef is with the giant Canada goose in the eastern states, because it just doesn't belong here. The geese sit in enormous flocks on undersized ponds and lakes year-round, fouling them with droppings. Most of them don't migrate, and they gradually ruin the habitat for a lot of other species.

There are either five or eight subspecies of Canada goose (*Branta canadensis*), depending on which biologist you ask.

The widest-spread variety is now the giant Canada goose, but it wasn't always so. The giant is a prairie native that once migrated north in warm weather and south in cold. It can weigh more than twenty pounds at maturity. It boggles the mind that the bird can get into the air at all.

Giant Canadas were hunted and pushed out of their native range to such an extent that for a time they were thought to be extinct. In 1962, a flock was discovered on a lake in Minnesota, but wild goose populations across the United States were low throughout the 1960s.

When biologists wanted to increase goose populations around the country, they selected the giant Canada goose as the species to run with. It's not clear why they didn't simply replenish and protect the species and subspecies that were indigenous to each region. Giant Canadas were bred in captivity for a few generations to increase their numbers, and then the stocking began.

People soon noticed something funny about these stocked giant Canada geese. They didn't fly south for the winter. They didn't seem to fly *anywhere* for the winter. Sometimes, perhaps when they felt the need to do something, they'd gather into important-looking V formations that didn't go anywhere in particular. Perhaps they'd fly a few miles down the road to the next lake. Or they'd fly in circles before landing exactly where they'd started.

These geese had no migratory tradition. Canada geese that are born in the wild learn migratory routes and timetables from older geese, usually their parents. Born in captivity and released far from their native range, these geese had no idea where they were supposed to go. So they didn't go anywhere.

Some of the geese were stocked in areas that had never seen a Canada goose in the first place. A lot of geese found themselves in places where human habitation had transformed the ecosystem and removed most of the natural predators. Bald eagles were once their major predators, but their numbers and range had been reduced to a fraction of what they'd been, through a combination of DDT, loss of nesting habitat, hunting, and lead poisoning.

As it happens, in most of North America, Canada geese don't have to migrate anyway. There's plenty of food where they are, year-round.

Geese are herbivorous, but inefficient at it. For their mass, grasses and aquatic plants have relatively little available energy. Most dedicated grass-eaters have an enormous digestive system that is designed to wring as much energy as possible out of every mouthful. You might think of a cow as a huge digestive system, its limbs and large body there to support a rumen, a stomach, and many meters of intestine. Slice open a deer and you'll see that the mass of a full rumen constitutes most of the torso. It takes a long, slow digestive system to extract much energy from a meal of grass.

Unlike cattle and deer, the giant Canada goose must be able to get off the ground. Because of this, its digestive process can't be so elaborate as to prevent it from flying. Over time, it has evolved to solve this problem: Unlike most other grass-eaters, it pushes plant matter through its digestive system as quickly as possible in order to make room for more. Its digestive system may be inefficient, but the giant Canada makes up for it in volume.

Like most other birds, Canada geese often excrete when they take flight, in order to reduce weight. The speed with which geese need to digest their food, and their inefficiency at doing this (relative to other grass-eaters) is why goose poop is usually green: The goose's digestive system is so rudimentary that there's still plenty of chlorophyll in there. Pound for pound, a goose must eat more plants to support itself than does any documented terrestrial mammal. When you park a flock of these birds unnaturally on the shore of a pond year-round, the detrimental effect on the ecosystem is severe.

To compound the problem, because so many natural predators have disappeared, the survival rate among goslings is much higher than what can be sustained without an impact on the local environment. Three hundred years ago, a pair of geese were probably lucky to have one or two survivors among their young each year, to follow them on their migration. Today it's not uncommon for half a dozen goslings to mature out of a clutch of suburban resident geese.

Thus, instead of a pond surrounded by forest, hosting a pair of geese that show up every year, stay awhile to raise a few goslings, then migrate, now that pond ecosystem (surrounded by grass and urbanization) must endure the presence of dozens of adult geese year-round — geese that eat the vegetation and poop it into the water, causing bacterial blooms and algal explosions.

Don't get me wrong; I'm delighted that the giant Canada goose dodged a bullet and hasn't gone extinct. But enough is enough. There are too many of them in places where they don't belong. And, just as with other invasive species wreaking havoc, this situation was caused by humans. As a human being myself, I see it as our collective responsibility to fix what we broke.

One remedy is to eat the invaders. Geese could easily be a delectable food source; each one contains from three to fifteen pounds of meat. Giant Canada geese are plentiful and ubiquitous. Somehow, though, people have trouble seeing them as food.

I had hunted and cooked Canada geese before, and knew they make for good eating. Then, one summer, I read an article in the *New York Times* explaining that the resident geese of Prospect

Park, in Brooklyn, would be rounded up, gassed, and deposited in a landfill. I was furious. Killing any animal is a serious thing, and the *wasteful* killing of anything is reprehensible. Using something as food at least gives meaning to its death.

The cull of Prospect Park's geese didn't come out of the blue. On January 15, 2009, a US Airways passenger jet hit a flock of geese and several birds were sucked into the engines, causing total engine failure. Captain Chesley B. "Sully" Sullenberger landed the plane on the Hudson River, saving the lives of all one hundred and fifty-five souls on board. It was called "the miracle on the Hudson," and rightfully recognized as a testament to good leadership and the human spirit.

While the rest of the United States was celebrating Captain Sullenberger, the Federal Aviation Administration started examining the goose situation that had caused not only the failure of Sully's engines but also several other accidents. Although isotope analysis was not able to determine conclusively whether the geese were migratory or resident, the FAA decided it was time to act.

It pushed for a cull of hundreds of thousands of geese in New York, especially around airports. Although other bird species result in a greater overall percentage of bird strikes, Canada geese are so big that they're considered more destructive to an engine in midflight. The FAA partnered with the USDA to study the possibility of reducing the numbers of geese on the ground near airports. The USDA began work on behalf of New York City–area airports by rounding up the geese of Prospect Park in an unannounced raid.

THROWING PERFECTLY GOOD GOOSE MEAT into a landfill rubbed me the wrong way, so I decided to do something about it. I e-mailed my contacts at Slow Food NYC, for whom I had recently conducted a series of events, with an offer to put on a “Slow Geese” workshop, in which I would speak about the issue of geese while cooking and serving wild goose. If the state of New York did not believe that wild Canada goose was edible, then I would prove it by offering a plate to anyone who cared to try it.

Slow Food is an international organization devoted to the antithesis of fast food. Founded in Italy, it comprises hundreds of “convivia” (a fancy word for “chapters”) in cities around the world. Members are dedicated to preserving traditional foodways and ingredients. Such as wild geese. Doing a Slow Geese presentation in the wake of the miracle on the Hudson made sense.

My friends at Slow Food agreed, and set a date in late October. They even booked a venue in Brooklyn within walking distance of Prospect Park. All I had to do was show up with some wild giant Canada goose to cook with a skilled chef and be prepared to talk to a bunch of Brooklynites about how they could become locavore hunters and get some geese of their own.

Now I just needed to bag a few geese; after all, I couldn’t do a cooking demo without the main ingredient. Like many other states, Virginia has a special September goose season with generous limits. In September, any migratory geese haven’t arrived yet, so it’s a safe assumption that any goose killed is a resident.

There are three primary strategies for hunting the Canada goose: hunting from a blind, pass shooting, and jump shooting.

Hunting from a blind is the approach most people are familiar with. First the hunter builds a blind near a large body of water. He (or she) then spreads an array of floating decoys on the surface of the water. The hunter is awake at a ridiculously early hour and ready in his blind, freezing his butt off, waiting for sunrise.

I've never engaged in that type of goose hunting: I like to sleep late, thanks. Nor can I afford the dozens of decoy geese this approach requires.

However, I have a lot of experience with the other types of goose hunting. Pass shooting is easy and fun. Rather than spending twenty dollars on a goose call, I practice making its sound with my own voice. I've had excellent success calling in flocks of geese with nothing but my hand and my mouth. I look for a big field with relatively short grass, which is where geese usually land to graze during September and October. (Geese won't commit to landing in tall grass, for fear of lurking predators, such as you.) I wait there until I hear geese honking in the distance. Most of the time I don't bother to hide — nonmigratory geese in my area are rarely hunted and so are wonderfully unsophisticated. If I imitate the call well, they'll fly straight in for me, and I ready myself to shoot as they descend.

The third type of goose hunting, called jump shooting, is the practice of finding a place where geese are already on the ground, scaring them at close range, and then shooting them as they fly off. This can be done on land or along water, though on water is more common.

I'd done plenty of pass shooting and jump shooting for geese on ponds, so I decided to try jump shooting on a river to bag my New York City–bound geese. The Rivanna River, which is close to my home in Albemarle County, Virginia, flows past several high-end housing developments whose residents complain vociferously about the geese yet wring their hands about the ethics of hunting. I thought I'd enjoy shooting a few geese as I floated in a canoe past the reflections of their enormous and expensive homes. As long as I was on the river, I'd be within the law.

So there I was, in a canoe on the river, once again accompanied by my father-in-law, Bob. We thought these resident geese would be so accustomed to being fed bread by hand that we'd be able to get close to them before they spooked. In practice, though, this isn't what happened.

The geese seemed to know the difference between guys in a canoe on a river with shotguns and, say, parents and their children on a pond with a loaf of bread. We would round a bend, spot some geese, and start paddling, and they'd take off before a shot was fired. After a few miles of this, I decided that rounding the bend was the problem. The canoe was too visible during that final approach.

To improve things, Bob and I stopped on a sandbar near the next serious bend in the river. Then, I could move as stealthily as possible on foot to see if there were geese waiting on the other side. We went many miles, stopping at various spits of land so I could test my theory.

At last, it worked. I left the boat and stepped cautiously and quietly, as though hunting deer, in my felt-soled water shoes. Heel to toe, each step. I parted the grass and peered over at a flock of several dozen geese on the water very nearby.

This presented a dilemma. Conventional "Marquess of Queensbury" rules of hunting waterfowl state that one must never ever shoot at a duck or goose on the water or on land (this is convention — not law). A hunter is supposed to wait until the goose has started to fly away before opening fire. As a public advocate for hunting for food and for removing invasive species, I never thought of myself as particularly concerned with that sort of thing. After all, the idea isn't to make it "sporting"; it's to solve an ecological problem. Yet I had absorbed too much of the traditional ethic. I stood there with my twelve-gauge Mossberg 500 pump-action shotgun in my hands and couldn't will myself to shoot at these geese on the water.

Okay, something had to be done.

"Hey, geese!" I yelled.

That did it. The flock beat their wings and launched their heavy, plant-eating bodies into the air. I picked out the closest one and squeezed the trigger. The bird dropped and I picked out another and shot it as well. I looked for a third within range, but they were higher now and passing the treetops. And then they were simply gone.

I looked back at the water for my geese and saw both of them swimming hard. I had hit them but not well enough, as they could still at least swim, if not fly. There was nothing for it but to go after them, gun and all. That's the beauty of hunting with an inexpensive pump-action shotgun: You can get it wet and dirty, and it will usually take a beating and live to shoot another day, even if it is a little uglier for the experience. And if it breaks, you can just buy another one.

I dived into the water and swam after the escaping birds. The ground level dropped quickly and soon I was in deep water. I felt mud under my feet again after a while and used the butt of the shotgun as a sort of bargepole to push myself off the bottom and advance more quickly. I floated down rapids and spun through white water that would have been minor in a canoe or kayak but posed a lot more trouble on foot with a shotgun in tow. Never did my Outward Bound white-water training serve me better.

The geese began to lose ground — not so much because of my prowess with a shotgun in white water but rather because they'd been shot with said shotgun, which is why they were swimming and not in flight. Had I been hit with the same dose of steel shot, I'd have dropped out long ago.

I caught up with the first goose and prepared to finish it off with the gun before realizing that:

A) This shotgun and its ammunition had just swum down a quarter mile of white water and might not shoot at all.

B) Even if it did manage to go *bang*, at a range of less than three yards there wouldn't be anything left to eat.

I drew closer to the angry, hissing goose and remembered that, as always, I had a knife in my pocket. The blade came out and the goose and I were *mano-a-*wing briefly before *mano* won the day and the goose was subjugated. Then I came up on the other goose on the opposite bank. It fought harder and I couldn't get the knife close to its neck. Dropping the knife, I grabbed the goose with both hands and dragged it under the water until neither of us could bear it any longer. I rose and took a breath, but the goose was dead.

More-experienced goose hunters have told me that what I just described is never, ever supposed to happen. Rather, expensive and well-trained retrievers are supposed to see to everything after the first few shots hit. I don't understand why these hunters are letting the dogs have all the adventure.

With the geese in hand, I was able to do the goose-cuisine demonstration in Brooklyn just before Halloween. I took Amtrak from Charlottesville to Manhattan with my frozen geese thawing in my suitcase. I stayed in Brooklyn, on my friend Caroline's couch. We painted the town red on the eve of the goose event; we must have had at least two drinks at every brownstone between the East Village and Park Slope. I fell asleep on the floor with one of her cats on my head, maybe two hours before I had to wake up.

Caroline managed to get me up and out of the apartment on time by pouring coffee down my throat. I was almost human when I checked in to the kitchen at a culinary learning center and dropped the geese on the counter for my friend Leighton to start prepping. I stumbled into the bathroom there and stared at myself in the mirror. Bloodshot eyes. Dark circles. At least I'd miraculously managed to shave.

Somehow, when I was about to start my presentation, forty-five minutes later, I'd been cured of the hangover from hell. The moment it was time to start talking, I came to life and found myself running at one hundred percent. Good thing, too; we had a full house.

I carved up the geese, then talked about hunting and butchering while Leighton cooked. Leighton bears more than a passing resemblance to Jeff Bridges's character, the Dude, from the film *The Big Lebowski.* The goose meat came out perfectly. Our audience enjoyed it enough that whatever scraps remained were claimed afterward. One older gentleman wanted a neck for stock, a young woman took home a spare goose breast, and one guy asked for all of the feet. I haven't the slightest idea what anyone would want with goose feet, but I gave them to him.

People seem to have two ideas in their heads about eating geese. First, there's a vaguely Dickensian image of an all-afternoon ordeal required to produce one meal (generally at Christmas). Even if goose tastes all right, the feeling is that you have to spend all day to get there. Other people believe wild goose will taste gamy and be tough, and isn't worth bothering with.

With all meat, age matters. A young example of a species will be tenderer than an old one. If you're stuck with an old bird, there are steps you can take to tenderize it, or you can process it differently. As with any kind of cooking, really, recognize what you have and deal with it appropriately. Because I'm hunting for food, I'm after a younger turkey, deer, or goose instead of an older, larger one that would make a good trophy.

Gaminess is usually the product of sloppy butchering rather than the fault of the meat, although with some animals, it can't be helped. For example, a fully mature, uncastrated boar almost always tastes foul. But for the most part, *gamy* is a catch-all term for meat that has been butchered badly. Usually it means the hunter took too long to get the meat carved off and then cooled to prevent bacterial contamination. This is a simple matter to deal with when hunting geese; I bring along a cooler full of ice and gut each goose as soon as possible.

The wonderful thing about hunting giant Canada geese for food is that you get so much for the effort. Many states have a special September hunting season during which resident geese are targeted. Bag limits are usually high, often up to half a dozen per day. There's more than the meat, too; the down is excellent stuff and comes out easily by the fistful. I've gotten into the habit of bringing an extra bag when I'm after geese so I can save the down in it. To kill any parasites, put the down in a cloth bag, stitch it closed, and run it through the dryer on high heat. A goose-down pillow requires just a few geese, or you can improve an inexpensive winter parka by removing the polyester filling and replacing it with wild-goose down, which is much warmer and resists damp.

The Slow Food cooking demo in Brooklyn received a good amount of press, and I repeated it back home in Virginia, this time at a winery and with a different group of chefs. Everyone thought the geese were worth eating. The only problem was that New York was still dumping its geese in landfills.

Months went by and I'd just about given up hope of changing anything. Suddenly, at the moment I least expected it — on the very evening when I got home from my long, strange hunt for nutria in Louisiana — I learned that New York City had finally relented. It would be sending its thousands of culled geese to Pennsylvania, to be donated to food banks.

Tilapia,

Plecos, and Armored Catfish

AFTER THE NUTRIA ODYSSEY, I wanted something uncomplicated for my next hunting trip. Learning about Philippe's successes in creating a market for nutria piqued my interest in other invasive species that could be moved onto grocery shelves and restaurant menus.

It would help to focus on something people were already comfortable eating, such as tilapia.

Tilapia is a fish known for its somewhat bland and unfishy flavor. It's a fish for people who don't especially like fish. It's widely available in grocery stores because it's easy to farm. In fact, genetic testing has shown that quite a lot of what is sold as another species of fish is tilapia: It's been fraudulently passed off as everything from Chilean sea bass to cod.

The simplicity of farming tilapia has led to its use in aquaculture around the world, in places far from its natural habitat in Africa and the Middle East — places like Florida.

Tilapia is actually a catch-all name for many dozens of species that belong to the Cichlidae family. Cichlids are popular for home aquariums, for a couple of reasons. First, they're good parents (as fish go). They care for their young longer than most other fish do, giving them an advantage over less doting parents that don't watch out for their offspring. Second, cichlids hybridize readily — that is, they'll mate with other species, occasionally creating a new breed.

The invasive tilapia started out as *Oreochromis aureus,* the "blue tilapia," which was introduced into the wild by the state of Florida in 1961. It was hoped the blue would become a popular game fish and also would devour some of the unsightly algae on Florida's lakes. It was assumed that Florida's largemouth bass would keep tilapia numbers in check.

In practice, blue tilapia were aggressive enough and grew fast enough to hold their own against the native bass. They multiplied rapidly and expanded their range beyond the lakes via the state's vast system of canals. According to Duane Chapman, a fish biologist with the U.S. Geological Survey who specializes in invasive fish, enough tilapia farms have been flooded (by hurricanes) and enough aquarium hobbyists have dumped unwanted fish that, because of their rather loose mating habits, there probably aren't many pure *Oreochromis aureus* left in Florida.

When I think of Florida and invasive species, my mind makes a beeline to George Cera, with whom I'd hunted black spiny-tailed iguanas the previous summer. George and I had kept in touch, and I was a guest on his radio talk show a few times. We talked on the phone now and then and kept up with each other's adventures. Because he knows wildlife inside and out and shares my passion for going after invasive species, he'd be the best guy in Florida to join me in pursuit of invasive fish.

I called him on a Thursday, right after returning from an outdoor writers conference in Utah. My suitcase was still packed. Our conversation went like this:

"Hey, George, you want to throw cast nets in canals next week and see what's really going on with the tilapia down your way? Maybe we can bag some other stuff while we're at it."

"Okay, but I need a guest in the studio on my radio show at eleven on Saturday morning. Can you make it?"

"That's a two-day drive . . ."

"Yeah, but I really need you on the air here."

"Okay, then."

A few hours later I was in the car, driving south as the sun went down. I think I got as far as North Carolina before I realized that my suitcase was packed for the snow-covered peaks at a ski resort in Utah rather than the muggy heat of Florida in July. Oh, well; too late.

I arrived at the studio with half an hour to spare. We did the show and then drove out to Gasparilla Island, where I checked into a lovely cottage that the good people of the Gasparilla Innlet had furnished for my use during the off-season.

The cottages at the Innlet are actually old houses of the classic local style: low, single-story cottages with hip roofs and a generous front porch. Each has been divided into four luxurious units, each with a private entry. It feels cozy and private, but in reality there could be someone on the other side of the wall from you.

After settling in, I went over to George's place, a few blocks away. We decided to get right to fishing. My car was already filled with gear of every description to meet any invasive-fish contingency, from crab traps to surf rods. George got in and we drove to the mainland at the edge of the Myakka River State Park.

Tilapia are primarily plant-eaters, so they don't often see a reason to bite a hook. This makes netting the most practical way of catching them. Fortunately, I had brought a small cast net of three or four feet in diameter.

A cast net is round, with weights around the edges and a long rope attached to the middle of it. You throw it in such a way that it spreads out in midair and sinks quickly when it hits the water. In addition to making it sink on top of any fish immediately, the weights close the net around any prey as it's lifted when you hoist the rope.

The first spot we tried was beside a small bridge over a canal. A bridge is a good place to fish in hot, sunny weather because fish seek its shade. Taking care to loop the end of the rope around my wrist (to use to raise the net), I threw what was surely the worst toss of a cast net George had ever seen.

George demonstrated the correct way to gather and throw the net. Holding a weight in each hand, you rotate your upper body to put a spin on the net and, through centripetal force, make it spread out fully.

"Throw it like it owes you money," he said.

That was good advice. I tossed that net as hard as I could. After a while, it started coming back in with fish. At first I was getting little native sunfish and baby bass. Then the darndest thing was flopping around in the net as I brought it up onto shore.

An armored catfish.

It was covered in what appeared to be an overlapping series of vertical plates along the length of its body. If you enlarged it to the size of a Greyhound bus, this fish would look like something out of the Devonian period. As it stood, the fish was about eight inches.

Armored catfish have been popular in home aquariums for years. They're native to the Amazon Basin, which is a tough neighborhood. If a fish can make it there, it can make it anywhere, given warm enough water. Armored catfish go by the name *Callichthys callichthys,* but scientists suspect that what's called *C. callichthys* in the aquarium trade is actually many similar but distinct species yet to be sorted out by taxonomists.

Not much research has been conducted on the impact of armored catfish on native Floridian wildlife. The one thing that's well established is that the fish cause problems for endangered manatees. During cold weather (cold for Florida), the manatee must keep still for long stretches of time, economizing calories by limiting movement. Studies show that armored catfish bug the hell out of the manatee when it's immobile. The catfish startles it and attempts to suck algae off its body. This prompts movement just when the animal needs to be staying still.

My own captured armored catfish struggled longer out of the water than any other fish I've ever caught, with the exception of American eels. I believe, contrary to many other people, that fish can experience pain; because of this, I always try to dispatch a fish as quickly as possible to avoid prolonged suffering. What I do is slide a knife very deep between the eyes and rock it back to the rear of the eyes. This pierces and disables the brain.

The trouble in this case was that the knife wouldn't go in. At all. I opened my backpack and pulled out a much bigger knife, one verging on Crocodile Dundee territory. That, too, failed to penetrate.

They don't call these things "armored" catfish for nothing.

Frustrated, I set the fish in the bottom of a cooler, hoping that it would expire soon.

After a while, George and I drove on a bit. That's the thing about throwing a cast net: The act of throwing it disturbs the fish in the area, so there's no point in repeatedly throwing it at the same spot. You make a few tosses and then move down the bank.

George knew of a spot that was usually loaded with tilapia. After a good rain, he said, you could see the grass at the edge of the water rustling from their movement. This spot would be great, he promised. It had only one catch.

Alligators. Many, very big alligators. Apparently the Myakka River State Park is notorious for them. These beasts made the gators I'd been dodging in Louisiana look like skinks. We stood against the disturbingly low railing of the bridge and watched a couple of nine-footers cruise in from a hundred yards away and make a beeline for the water directly under us.

These alligators have seen people with cast nets, and know a dangling net on a rope promises a meal at each end. George helpfully pointed out that it would be necessary here to tie the rope to the bridge rather than looping it around my wrist. One good tug from a nine-foot alligator and I'd be in the water on top of it (at best).

The alligators were a definite problem. I would move from spot to spot on the railing, throw the net, and watch as gators swam for it, hoping it would be full of fish and worth tearing apart. Their very movement into the area scared away the fish. We had to constantly move from one spot to another. On several occasions, one particularly aggressive gator grabbed the net or the rope in its mouth and refused to let go. There wasn't much to do except wait and take pictures until it tired of this game.

The sun began to set and the park would be closing soon. Some bold armadillos sauntered across the road in full view. If hunting had been allowed in the park, I'd have gone after them. We weren't quite skunked, with one armored catfish bagged, and felt good about our prospects for the next day. I drove George home and then went back to my cottage.

I sat outside on the concrete steps and opened the cooler. To my surprise, the catfish seemed none the worse for wear. I discovered later that the armored cat normally gulps air, as many other catfishes do. It has dense capillaries lining the inside of its stomach that absorb oxygen in a manner similar to the working of a lung.

One way or another, I had to kill, gut, clean, and freeze the fish for cooking at another time (I had a fridge and a microwave but no stove or oven). I tried again to pierce the brain. It only seemed to encourage the fish, which slipped out of my grasp and into a flowering shrub. I crawled in to retrieve it.

Decapitation is never how I want to kill a fish because, among other reasons, I like to cook a small fish whole in order to get more meat out of it. Nevertheless, out of desperation, I tried it. If anything, the plates where I attempted to cut were even tougher than they were between the eyes.

I had one more trick. Using the back of my hatchet, I gave the fish's head a mighty thump. It lay still.

Satisfied that the fish was dead, I pondered how to gut it. It turned out that the softer, lighter-colored underside was penetrable by a very sharp, short knife. It was still tough as leather, but penetrable.

I've often wondered what the natural advantages are of having a soft white underbelly. We find it in many species from fish to mammals. That soft white underbelly seems to be the undoing of many kinds of animals. Yet there must be some advantage to it, or nature wouldn't repeat herself this way. The most likely explanation, in my opinion, is that soft white underbellies appear in nature because they can exist in a typically inaccessible part of the anatomy without significant danger to the organism. No bones, armor, or thick hide to waste nutrients on growing or maintaining; no coloration for camouflage or communication with other animals. I imagine that in a state of perfect grace, with no need to fight, run, or hide, most species would become sort of flabby pale blobs. It would be soft white underbelly all around.

After the fish was mostly gutted, I lifted my head and immediately regretted the fish guts I saw strewn over the beautifully manicured lawn. I reminded myself to clean them up later. I looked around for something to rinse the fish with, but there was no spigot. Well, the job would have to be finished under the sink in the bathroom.

I was carrying the mostly gutted fish to the immaculate white bathroom, along with the somewhat bloody hatchet, when suddenly it exploded back to life. The armored wonder jerked and flopped out of my hands and sailed through the air, sending a fine spray of bright red blood and guts all over the wall and floor in a pretty fair impression of Jackson Pollock's better-known work.

The fish then launched itself from the floor back into the air and against the wall. I lunged for it, slipped, and bumped my head painfully against the base of the sink.

"Goddammit, just die already!" I shouted.

I thumped against the opposite wall and grabbed the flailing zombie fish with both hands. Now I was mad.

"You're dead!" I shouted at the fish. "Accept it! It's over!"

The fish flopped out of my hands and this time landed in the bathtub.

"Fine, stay there. Go ahead, lie down in the bathtub and die!"

I stood panting in the doorway, bloody hatchet in hand, surveying the spattered wall. This is when I heard other guests' voices through the wall behind me. And if I could hear them, they could hear me.

Quickly, I tried to recall everything I'd learned from the only two episodes of *CSI* I'd ever seen. How long until the cops show up? How long will they listen to me babbling about an undead fish before arresting me, handcuffing me, throwing me in jail, and searching for a body?

First the murder weapons. I rinsed the hatchet and knives and stashed them in my suitcase. The bathroom didn't have to look perfect. Just good enough for a quick once-over. Like the car in *Pulp Fiction*. Then I turned my attention to the walls. The blood was already drying. Not good.

I spent the next several hours scrubbing every surface of that white bathroom until the evidence was gone. Well, except for the shower curtain, which, I'm afraid, will never be its old self again.

Somehow the police never showed up. The best explanation I could think of was that the people next door were too concerned about a corpse of their own to call the cops.

THE NEXT MORNING, for breakfast, I gorged myself on mangoes from George's yard. (He grows three or four varieties within a few steps of each other. I don't think I've ever eaten a piece of fruit as good as that first mango, fresh off the tree.) Then we headed out for another round of net-fishing.

We found another little bridge in the mainland town of Rotonda. I threw the net for a while without coming up with anything but native fishes. Then I found something in there with the bluegill and minnows that surprised me.

A plecostomus.

Hypostomus plecostomus is ubiquitous in freshwater home aquariums; you've no doubt seen them. Plecos are those sucker fish in the catfish family that people put in their tanks to clean the algae off the sides. They do a good job and will eventually become enormous. I kept aquariums at home for years and had a pleco that grew to almost a foot long — too big for the tank. I gave it to a friend who had a bigger aquarium, which is one of the three things people eventually do with them. The other two? They're euthanized or they're released into the wild by those who just can't kill what they've come to think of as pets.

I sympathize with that. I wouldn't want to kill a pet, either. In fact, it was strange to have this thing in my net that looked as if it came from a pet store. The trouble with releasing a fish from an aquarium is that if it survives, it may breed. With tropical fish released in an area as warm as Florida, odds are good of an invasive fish living long enough in the wild to reproduce. That's what happened with plecos in parts of Florida, and around the world as well.

Like the armored catfish, the pleco is native to the Amazon Basin. It evolved in the presence of some of the fiercest freshwater predators on earth. It's a well-camouflaged bottom dweller that's built like a tank and grows big enough to be left alone by all but the most voracious predators. In the wild, some have been found as long as four feet.

George told me that the pleco in the net was no fluke. They're in the canals and lakes in great numbers, but not much research has been conducted regarding their ecological impact. Because they're usually not tempted by anything a fisherman uses as bait, you can work a body of water for years without any idea that plecos are there. Also, their bottom-dwelling habit makes it unlikely that they'll be adequately represented in an electrofishing survey.

Plecos have wiped out entire commercial fisheries. An invasive population in El Presa Infiernillo, a reservoir in Mexico, outcompeted the catch the local fishermen depended on for survival and ruined the fishing for years. Ironically, what were lost were the tilapia.

I had never heard of anyone eating a pleco. But since my interest lies in determining whether invasive species could be used as food, this pleco would be a meal.

For now, though, we had to get serious about tilapia. I was content with bagging two new invasive species in as many days, but the primary reason for my journey to Florida still eluded us. George suggested that we hit the golf courses, which are notorious reservoirs of tilapia in Florida. Heavy fertilization of the turf runs off into the water hazards, leading to abnormally huge algal blooms and aquatic-plant growth. This in turn provides a lot of food for more tilapia than would otherwise be supported by a pond or water-filled ditch of any size.

George is known in the region for his work with invasive iguanas and for his radio show, so I let him do the talking when we went into the first clubhouse. The guy at that counter didn't think that there were many tilapia in the ponds there but directed us to a sister course he swore was loaded with them.

When we tried that second clubhouse, we were told that the first place was the hot spot. We probably could have spent all day going back and forth, but instead I explained to the staff what we were trying to do. They were all for it and even offered us the use of a golf cart.

You hear stories about people getting in trouble for fishing on a golf course without permission. It's best to ask; sooner or later, one of them will say yes. Dress like a golfer, ask nicely, follow the rules (never drive a cart across the green, for example), and never leave any trash on the course. In our case, I think they liked that we were using a cast net exclusively, meaning there'd be no lost lures or hooks to injure humans or wildlife.

We started hitting ponds and canals around the course. (To my relief, we didn't see many alligators.) It wasn't long before I hit pay dirt. I hauled up the net and in it was a big, flopping, silvery-bluish fish, which I stared at without recognition.

"What the hell is that?" I asked George, incredulously.

"A tilapia," he said, as if I'd asked the most ridiculous question in the world.

The nutria experience was still heavy on my mind, so the last thing I expected to see was what I was looking for.

It began to rain steadily. I put the tilapia on ice with the pleco, and we returned to George's place on Gasparilla Island.

"I'M NOT GONNA EAT THAT THING," George insisted, looking at the pleco I'd laid out next to the tilapia on a picnic table in his backyard.

Well, I'd heard that line before. Turn it into food, though, and people's minds change.

The first step was gutting and scaling. With the tilapia, the procedure was straightforward. It was much like a bass or a bluegill, aside from the larger and longer digestive tract typical of an herbivore.

When it came to the pleco, though, I had to do things differently. At first I gutted it, but I quickly saw that in a pleco this size (nine inches), all of the meat is in the tail. I made a diagonal cut to separate the fleshy back end from the front. Scaling it was out of the question. The skin is tough and leathery, and the scales reminded me of the scutes on a snapping turtle. The scales didn't look like they were going anywhere. Might as well leave them.

Because tilapia is already widely accepted as a food source, I thought it would be a good idea to cook the tilapia and the pleco side by side, using the same recipe, and then do a taste test. I placed the whole, gutted tilapia on a piece of aluminum foil and the pleco tail on another piece. I picked up a mango knocked down by the wind, cut it into small pieces, and stuffed some into each fish. I poured the mango juice over the meat, as well as a little olive oil, then added some salt and a little black pepper.

I sealed each fish in the foil (I would have preferred to wrap them in grape leaves, but we didn't have any) and baked them at 350 degrees F until they were cooked through. To see if a whole fish is done, check out the eye: When it's fully white, the meat's about ready. My headless pleco was about the same thickness as the tilapia, so I used the one set of eyes to gauge both fish.

When they were done, even the pleco looked like real food. I offered George the first taste.

George looked at me doubtfully. He dipped a fork into the tilapia and had a bite. "Not bad. The mango makes it."

I tasted the tilapia as well. I found the flavor to be fine — it mostly tasted like mango and salt. Good, but nothing special. The texture was okay, but not as firm as I prefer. My attention moved to the pleco. I took a forkful from the bones and ate it.

The pleco was better. It had a firmer texture and a somehow cleaner flavor. George looked doubtful, but he finally tried it. This was the same guy who the previous summer had convinced me to eat iguana, so I suppose there was a bit of tit-for-tat.

"Wow! This is better than the tilapia," he said.

George agreed that both the flavor and the texture of the pleco were superior in every way to those of the tilapia. In fact, he finished the rest of the pleco and left only bones (easily avoided) and the husk of skin.

Invasive plecostomus could have real potential as food. It can be netted in large numbers, and baiting them with submerged vegetation the day before throwing a net could be an effective tactic. I've even seen pictures of thousands of netted plecos heaped up in trash piles in Mexico. It's a shame the people didn't eat the fish rather than dispose of them.

The tilapia could also be harvested en masse as a commercial food source by enterprising locals. Two people with a really wide gill net dragged through the water column (much more efficient than my little cast net) could probably net a thousand fish a day.

The market for tilapia is already established, and the fish could be sold without the overhead of building, stocking, and maintaining artificial ponds. Could wild-netted freshwater tilapia in Florida beat the prices of Chinese imports? I wonder.

George had to return to work and I had to leave for home the following afternoon. Still, we'd be able to squeeze in a little iguana hunting before I hit the road. I was curious about how the situation had changed since I'd last visited the island.

George had lost the town's contract as the official hunter of black spiny-tailed iguanas and then suddenly regained it shortly before I came to visit. The U.S. Department of Agriculture had arrived and convinced the town council to stop putting out the contract to bid and let the federal government take care of the iguanas instead.

The previous winter, I'd heard accounts of the USDA guys doing ridiculous things that eventually led to the town showing them the door. For example, they cruised the streets day after day in forty-degree weather pretending to hunt. At that temperature, the cold-blooded lizards retreat underground and become inactive. George's approach in cold weather had been to take a leave of absence without pay until the iguanas could be hunted again. Instead, the USDA men spent the public's money and burned gas for nothing.

It was a little more difficult to hunt them now, George said, as we cruised around in his golf cart. The USDA men had been hunting with .22 LR rifles loaded with conventional bullets, unlike the air rifles and .22 birdshot George favors. These are dangerous weapons with their deadly ammunition, yet the men had been seen shooting toward roads and houses, frightening people and occasionally causing property damage. Because of this, properties George had been given access to by landowners were now off-limits.

George stopped the cart in front of a lushly landscaped yard and shouldered his gun. I took a quick photo of a midsize male iguana about a half second before a shot to the head spun it around and left it twitching. I grasped it by the tail and smacked the head hard against the trunk of a coconut palm, just in case.

Anoles, a major food for the spiny-tails, were in shorter supply than they'd been last year. There are two species: the tiny brown, invasive Cuban anoles (*Anolis sagrei*) and the larger, native, green Carolina anoles (*Anolis carolinensis*). More spiny-tailed iguanas means fewer anoles, and thus more of the insects on the anoles' menu. I noticed that mosquito numbers were way up, although I don't know for sure that the reduction in anoles was why.

There were definitely a lot more big iguanas than I'd seen earlier, however — no doubt the result of a year of ineffective hunting and trapping before George was back in charge. The large females were a particular concern. Things would get worse before they got better, George said. Even though he'd been taking out the big females as fast as he could, their high numbers in the spring meant clutches of eggs were waiting to hatch in August, at which time there'd be a population boom.

The situation underscored to me what a difference one person can make. That George had singlehandedly changed the ecology of the island was incredible. I'd been there the year before, after he'd reduced the iguana population by sixteen thousand, and now I could see what happened after his work had been interrupted. One knowledgeable and dedicated hunter invested in the community and in the ecosystem can be more effective than any study or a big-budget federal agency. If people let down their guard, it takes just a few seasons for a species to rebound.

I doubt that every invasive iguana will ever be eradicated from Gasparilla Island. Nor will all of the tilapia and plecos be removed from the mainland's waterways. Steady, intensive hunting and fishing can, however, control the numbers enough to ensure the survival of the native wildlife for another year.

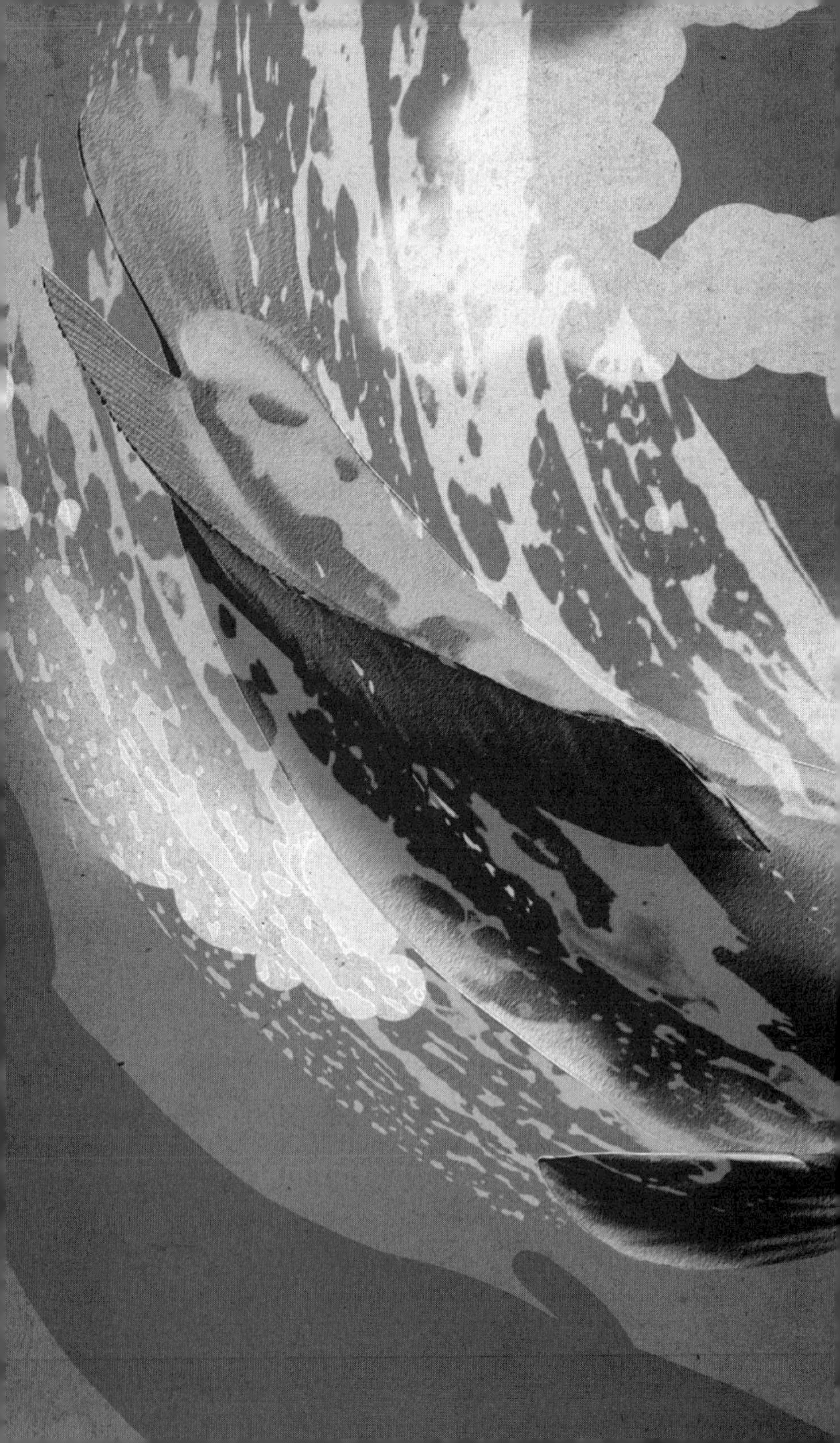

Snake-heads

I was becoming dangerously smug. On the very first cast I'd caught a fish! I could bring it in, kill it, put it on ice, and go home. Mission accomplished!

Only not so much. I had it in close enough that I could see it was definitely a snakehead. Then it did a sort of sideways flip, bit through the line, and disappeared. I was left with a sadly chomped-off length of fishing line and an open mouth.

My first thought was: I'm going to need a bigger rod.

If there's a poster child for invasive species in North America, it's the snakehead fish. In 2002, the first wild population was detected in a pond in Crofton, Maryland. Within days, the national media went crazy over the discovery, branding the invaders "Frankenfish." The species was bizarre to them because of its apparent lack of predators, sharp teeth, and its ability to survive for long periods on dry land. Some species of snakehead can grow to more than three feet long. The public's imagination quickly processed this information and imagined an enormous fish that would squirm out of the water, crawl over the ground, and kill pets or even human beings. Suddenly, people were terrified — so terrified that two horror movies were quickly produced to take advantage of the rampant fear of these fish.

Every invasive species is native somewhere, though, and understanding an animal begins with learning about where it came from. Snakeheads are a group of about thirty species of fish from different parts of Asia. They are sharp-toothed ambush predators that can accelerate rapidly. The species in Crofton, Maryland, is the northern snakehead (*Channa argus*). It doesn't get as big as the notorious giant snakehead (*C. micropeltes*), which many in the media incorrectly describe as being the problem. Although a few giant snakeheads have been caught in the wild in the United States, it's the northern snakehead that has established expanding breeding populations in the wild.

The snakehead has a clever and efficient design. It looks something like the native bowfin, with a long fin along the top. It has excellent camouflage (the colors are similar to a copperhead snake) and the ability to gulp air from the surface rather than depending on the absorption of dissolved oxygen in the water passing over its gills.

This air-gulping capacity enables snakeheads to survive in poor habitat with shallow water, where other fish would die. This adaptation may seem strange, but many other species of fish share the ability: Some catfish, for example, such as the invasive armored species I encountered in Florida, have it.

Somehow people overlooked the fact that the ability to gulp air was not exclusive to the snakehead, and this characteristic added to the hype surrounding the arrival of the northern snakeheads in Maryland. The result? The state of Maryland took brisk, serious action. It hit that pond with the most deadly chemicals it dared to use and then drained it.

Among the dead snakeheads were a pair of large adults and a great many young snakeheads, obviously a breeding population.

After Maryland's swift and decisive action, a game of Whac-A-Mole erupted in the area. Snakeheads were found to have already somehow ended up in the nearby Potomac River. Genetic analysis suggests that the snakeheads in the Potomac originated from a separate introductory event, one not related to how they got into the pond. It seems a strange coincidence that two sources dumped the same kind of fish, originating from the other side of the planet, into bodies of water only a few miles apart (especially a fish that most people had never heard of), but that's what scientists think happened.

Snakeheads actually weren't rare in the United States before we started hearing about them on the news. When I was in middle school (in Columbia, Maryland, near a tributary of the Potomac, as it happens), some of my friends were serious fish geeks. These boys could be divided into two groups: the kids whose parents let them have a fifty-five-gallon tank and those who were stuck with the limitations of ten-gallon aquarium. The ten-gallon kids were breeding small fish, such as bettas. The kids with the bigger tanks were into Brazilian arowanas and Asian snakeheads.

Even the guys with snakeheads seemed to start out with a ten-gallon setup. As the fish grew, though, they'd graduate to a much bigger tank. I remember seeing their six-inch snakeheads and marveling at the vigor with which they would tear apart a feeder goldfish only seconds after it was dropped into the tank. We all knew they'd eventually grow to be more than a foot and a half long, but that seemed far in an unimaginable future.

Even a fifty-gallon tank is a bit small for a fish pushing eighteen inches that will attack fish of equal size. And what would happen when those friends of mine went away to college? Or if they got bored with the hobby? Or their families moved someplace where a big aquarium wasn't allowed? No kid wants to kill his own pet.

Even I must admit to unleashing a nonnative species as a child. When I was fourteen, I went to a crawfish boil put on by a family friend. He had ordered a mess of Louisiana crayfish, alive and kicking, to be shipped to Virginia for what turned out to be a great party. At the end of the evening, there were a lot of live crayfish left. I brought home a few dozen in a bag and obliviously dumped them into a pond next to our house. I was doing them a favor, I thought. Of course, being just a kid, I knew nothing about the danger of invasive species. Today, descendants of those crayfish are still in my parents' pond (and who knows how far downstream).

EVENTUALLY A LOCAL MAN who had purchased snakeheads for food confessed to dumping them in that pond in Maryland, having tired of keeping them in an aquarium.

Purchasing a live fish for food may seem strange to most Americans, but among certain immigrant populations this is not uncommon. In China and Korea, snakeheads are a traditional food, and Asian markets often keep a tank of them. In parts of Asia, people believe that eating fresh snakehead can help someone recover more quickly from surgery, and the fish is valued as much for its role in medicine as in food. In the United States, until the brouhaha in Maryland, there were no restrictions on the importation or sale of live snakeheads. As a matter of fact, the fish's ability to gulp air made it easier than other fish to import live. Today it is illegal to import live snakeheads into the United States, though smuggling still occurs.

There are snakeheads of various species, mostly northerns, in Florida, with suspected breeding populations in California, Alabama, and Hawaii as well. Game wardens think many of these are the result of deliberate introduction by people involved in selling snakeheads for food. By dumping them into waterways, those purveyors would have a live source without having to pay to import them.

Some government authorities and scientists who study the fish or the local ecology doubt that northerns are established in Florida. My experience contradicts this, however. I've spoken with enough fishermen who have caught snakeheads, and have visited enough online forums of fishermen who work the canals of southern Florida, and seen enough photos posted online to believe those who say they're catching them on a daily basis. According to these fishermen, the conversation is no longer about how many snakeheads are around but rather about which hooks and lures are best to land the biggest trophies.

Once I decided to look for snakeheads to eat, naturally I wanted to see what was going on in the neighborhood of the most notorious introductions along the Potomac River. Both Maryland and Virginia (which share the Potomac) require that all snakehead catches be reported. I started researching where and by whom snakeheads had been caught.

The most recent government data I found indicates that no single fisherman on the Virginia stretch of the Potomac has ever caught more than two snakeheads in a season. This was disheartening. I knew the fish were out there and causing problems, but maybe it would be difficult to encounter one. There are plenty of retirees devoted to fishing who fish the upper Potomac several times a week. If they weren't getting more than two, what were the odds of my fishing for a few days — and with no boat — and getting a bite, let alone catching one? Officially, there were so few snakeheads caught in Virginia that they might as well not be there.

This made me put off going after the fish on the Potomac. I even considered making another trip to Florida, where I knew they were more plentiful (if less documented). Then one night in July, at about two in the morning, I was reading a blog and saw that a snakehead had been caught for the first time at Mason Neck State Park, which is in northern Virginia. I'd never heard of the park, so I looked it up and then mapped out directions. Less than twelve hours later, I was in the car and on my way north in search of snakeheads.

Mason Neck State Park closes at dusk and doesn't allow camping, so I had to find somewhere else to sleep in order to get to the park early in the morning. Only a few miles away is Pohick Bay Regional Park, operated jointly by several counties.

Campsites were available, so I went there first. I walked into the office and spoke with the young man behind the counter.

"Hi, I'm looking for snakeheads. Ever catch one around here?"

The kid looked befuddled, then collected himself.

"I don't do a whole lot of fishing myself, but I've seen people bring 'em in at the boat landing plenty. They catch 'em out on the river."

Now I was on to something. Snakeheads might officially be recent here, but it sure sounded as if they were a regular feature under the radar.

I paid for my campsite and left. After I'd pitched the tent, I went down a steep slope, carrying rod and tackle box, to the river.

Where it was possible, I walked along the river; much of the bank was too steep and tangled to approach. A trail ran roughly parallel to the bank through the woods, and I followed that until I reached a boat landing, its parking area full of trucks and trailers. A sign forbade fishing off the landing and from the dock, from which boats were rented on the weekend, and from anywhere else that might get a person even remotely close to a fish. All I had to do, though, was stand around the boat landing and make a nuisance of myself for a while, and then I got the good word about snakeheads.

A motley assortment of fishermen brought in their boats. When I asked them, they told me that, yes, they'd hooked snakeheads on the river from time to time. None of them had been after snakeheads and none had bothered to report his catch. One guy had actually thrown his fish back alive.

This sounded promising. I looked for a spot along the bank where I could cast past the many yards of green scum that floated near shore. Banned from the floating dock, I didn't have many options.

I considered what lure to use; despite the online forums, there hadn't been much information on the subject. Most people seemed to get snakeheads on bass fishing tackle, so I started with an old bass fisherman's standby, the red rubber worm.

A long cast sent it way out, and I began my retrieve as soon as it hit the water. I reeled slowly. When the worm was almost in, lying in the water no more than seven feet from me, a large blur dropped out of the sky from behind me and landed on the lure in a confusing mass of brown-and-white feathers.

I had no idea what was happening.

Then I realized that what I was looking at was an osprey that had pounced on my lure. I'd heard of clever ospreys learning to grab fish from lines as fishermen reeled them in, but rubber worms from a hook?

Great, I thought as the osprey flailed about at the end of the line, *I've caught myself an osprey and it's gotten itself hooked. I'll have to get it off somehow without getting my eyes gouged out or being ticketed by Fish and Wildlife.*

It struck the water and sent spray into my face, then it was back in the air, without carrying off either my rod or me. The hook was still in the water and the rubber worm was gone. I stared at the sky, slack-jawed, for at least a minute.

Sensible people would have found another place to fish. On the other hand, sensible people don't decide at two in the morning to drive for hours on I-95 to sleep in a tent and catch an invasive Frankenfish that had been reported only once in the area.

I kept fishing that spot. Half an hour later I had my first bite from something other than a federally protected raptor. It was a fish, though not a big one. I worked it in, not clear on when to set the hook. As it zigzagged its way toward shore, I saw its outline once it got to ten feet from the water's edge. The long dorsal fin suggested either a snakehead or a native bowfin.

Before I could determine what it was, once again a feathered torpedo hit the water and once again the son of a bitch nabbed what was on the hook and flew off with it before I could grasp what was happening. This one left the lure, though.

Sunset was approaching and the mosquitoes were coming out in force. I wound in my line and went back to my tent.

That night, my campsite was raided by a bunch of raccoons that stole a couple of crab traps, presumably for the sake of some leftover bits of chicken necks still clinging to the wire. In the morning, I looked for the traps but in vain. Those animals at Pohick Bay Regional Park are a bunch of thieves, and maybe liars and tax cheats, too.

After I broke camp, I drove the few miles to Mason Neck State Park, which I'd been aiming for all along, and parked near the nature center. A park ranger was walking toward his truck, and I quickly intercepted him.

Did he know anything about snakeheads in the area? Officer Timothy C. Smith told me I'd come to the right place, and he directed me to a pond some four hundred yards away.

This pond, he promised me, was full of snakeheads. People caught them now and then, but no other fish larger than a minnow swam in it. I asked him what kind of tackle people used, and he suggested a top-water lure that could be skipped over the plentiful muck and weeds.

All righty, then. I grabbed my gear and hauled it down to the pond. It was a small body of water, less than half an acre, but it was connected to the river via a small inlet, a stream of perhaps a dozen yards. At high tide this stream filled and the river washed into the pond. A sort of boardwalk ran along one side of the pond.

My rod was a light Shakespeare Uglystik with a cheap reel that I'd used for bass and bluegill, loaded with eight-pound test line. I rigged a wooden top-water lure with a couple of treble hooks on it and cast into the middle of the pond, home of the least amount of pond scum to snag the hooks.

Within a second, I had a great almighty bite. This fish nailed the lure with incredible force and ran with it like a tarpon. I was stunned at the ferocity with which something had grabbed the lure. This didn't feel like any largemouth bass I'd ever hooked.

The fish fought hard and I fought back. I strained at it, tightened up the drag, and cranked the reel. I was becoming dangerously smug. On the very first cast I'd caught a fish! I could bring it in, kill it, put it on ice, and go home. Mission accomplished!

Only not so much. I had it in close enough that I could see it was definitely a snakehead. Then it did a sort of sideways flip, bit through the line, and disappeared. I was left with a sadly chomped-off length of fishing line and an open mouth.

My first thought was: *I'm going to need a bigger rod.* Back in the car I only had one other fishing rig, my saltwater rod and reel, a nice Shimano Sonora 5000 on a stiff two-piece rod and loaded with a sixteen-pound test. Maybe the heavier line would hold up better . . . I wouldn't be able to cast that rod with precision, though.

The only top-water lure I'd brought was gone for good, so I spent the rest of the day fishing with various inappropriate lures with, not surprisingly, no luck. I saw plenty of snakeheads once the wind picked up and blew the pond scum to one side. Their long, prehistoric-looking, almost reptilian bodies were clearly visible when they basked near the surface.

Other than the snakeheads, I didn't see a single fish longer than two inches. Every fish that belonged in that pond was gone, except for smaller fry that had probably washed down in the stream that fed the pond or come in from the river at high tide. The only other moving life were thousands of tadpoles, hundreds of frogs, and dozens of turtles. Ominously, one of the turtles was missing a leg.

Tim, the park ranger, showed up to see how I was doing.

"What are these fish still doing here?" I asked. "Can't you get DGIF [the Department of Game and Inland Fisheries] or someone else to come in and electrofish them out?"

"We tried," Tim said with a sigh. "We put in a request to DGIF a year ago and they didn't want to come out. They just said to let people fish them out."

I couldn't believe what I was hearing.

"So you're saying the state knows this pond is here, full of snakeheads, and has decided to do nothing about it?"

"Pretty much."

I realized as the day wore on that I was badly armed. The situation called for a stiff, sturdy rod with a good reel, but lighter and with more finesse than my surf rod. I needed something that would let me cast carefully to avoid the tangles of weeds and the fallen tree mid-pond that snarled and stole lures from bad casts. I also needed a high-test line and steel leaders that could resist the sharp teeth of a snakehead. Finally, I needed weed-bucking top-water lures that wouldn't get tangled up on pond scum with every cast. The best look like what was probably a snakehead's favorite meal — a frog.

That day I was skunked, but I came away with good plan to land a snakehead. I made the long drive home and the next morning ordered a rod, a reel, and various accoutrements. A week later, I had a proper snakehead rig and again set out to land a snakehead.

I also did more research on the snakehead's feeding behavior. I wanted to know exactly how it hit a lure, its favorite foods, and when it was likely to be hungry. I'd fallen into the classic trap of the modern hunter or fisherman: So obsessed with gear, locations, and tactics, I hadn't focused on the animal itself.

There were scads of videos of snakeheads feeding in aquariums. I watched them repeatedly and noticed that a snakehead doesn't usually hit its prey in the same way a largemouth bass does. Like most fisherman from the southern and eastern parts of the country, I was stuck in the bass-fishing mind-set. A bass swallows its prey whole, in one big gulp. It has no teeth, nor does it need any. A snakehead will sometimes swallow small prey whole, but it's also willing to go after a meal that's far too big to gulp down. It's prone to grabbing the tail end of a prey animal with its sharp teeth and twisting its body rapidly in order to tear off a chunk. Deprived of a tail or hind legs, the victim probably isn't going anywhere. The snakehead then takes its time savoring the meal.

The pond I'd been fishing was perfect snakehead habitat. These fish don't care for an environment like the open water of the Potomac. As lunging ambush predators, they're built for a sudden burst of speed from thick cover. They prefer an area with thick weeds, tall grass, and vegetation so dense that you'd find it difficult to believe any fish could be in it.

In late spring and early summer, both snakehead parents will guard anywhere from a few dozen to hundreds of their small, bright-red young. Normally, a youngster needs good camouflage, but perhaps the bright color of a baby snakehead helps its parents keep track of and guard it. This advantage balances its increased visibility to predators. Any invader that approaches a young snakehead will be attacked viciously by the parents. This protective behavior accounts for many of the horror stories of snakehead attacks reported by the media.

Their habits as devoted parents can be exploited during the right season, though. That instinct to attack whether or not the parent fish is hungry makes it easy to catch during spawning season.

Unfortunately, I had arrived too late; the young were grown and had dispersed.

Once again I camped at Pohick Bay. I woke up at dawn to drive to Mason Neck. I brought an array of top-water lures to try out, including something called a Scum Frog.

After some experimentation, I found that the Scum Frog was the only lure in my tackle box to work. Now that I knew what sections of the pond the snakeheads were likely to haunt, I cast repeatedly into muck and snags I never would've imagined trying to fish. The Scum Frog has a pair of large hooks with their tips blocked by the soft rubber of the frog's body. A pair of rubber legs dangle behind. The design works well enough that I could drag the lure through muck without getting snagged and without having to remove the half a pound of weeds other lures brought in.

The hits began. I'd get a bite, move to set the hook, start bringing in the line, and in a flash the fish would be gone.

Park staff came to see what was going on with the crazy guy trying to catch snakeheads. They all had stories.

I was intrigued by the account of Trevor Via. As a land maintenance ranger at Mason Neck, he has spent a lot of time outside. Officially, if you recall, nobody in Virginia has caught more than two snakeheads within a calendar year. Trevor says he caught three in a single day out of that very pond, which must give him the state record, unofficial though it is.

On that day, Trevor caught the first of the three on a bare hook. The surface was mostly clear of duckweed and muck, and he could see a number of snakeheads hanging around near the surface. He cast, hoping to snag a fish through the side of the body and then drag it in. But he missed his mark. As he reeled in the line, the hook passed in front of a snakehead and the fish lunged at it. Trevor hooked that fish on a six-pound-test line with a light, whippy rod, and the battle was on.

His fight to land the snakehead would have been shorter if he'd had a heavier line. A thicker, stronger line makes it easier and faster to reel in a fish. In spite of its designation, however, it's possible to land a ten-pounder on six-pound line. The fight will take longer, and without some finesse on the part of the angler, the line can be broken.

Trevor said he spent a solid half hour fighting that snakehead all over the pond before managing to bring it to shore.

The park staff also busted a myth I'd heard time and again: that mature snakeheads in the United States don't have any predators. I spoke with people who said they watched as ospreys grabbed the adult fish from just beneath the water's surface. After what I witnessed of thieving ospreys a few miles away, I had no doubts. Even at the corner of the pond where I was fishing now, there's a tree with bare branches on which ospreys perch, looking down at the water in search of fish.

This predation is not heavy enough to stop the rapid expansion of snakeheads, but it's something. Perhaps in ten or twenty years ospreys and bald eagles will have evolved to specialize in hunting adult snakeheads.

I fished from various spots around the pond. Now and then, a snakehead would come up for an instant to gulp air or lunge at some type of prey. Usually this activity was near the shore or in waters surrounding a fallen tree. By midday, I started to notice some odd things. For example, the bullfrogs didn't act like bullfrogs. Usually, when you approach one by the water's edge in daylight, it jumps into the water when you get close. These frogs didn't do that. I could get to within five feet before they bolted. It was as if they thought whatever was waiting for them in the water was more dangerous than I was.

At around two, I was watching a goldfinch perched on a branch of the mostly submerged tree in the center of the pond. I took a few pictures, then it flitted to another twig only a few inches from the surface. The water suddenly erupted. Something big and dark seized the goldfinch and disappeared under the water.

Videos of snakeheads in aquariums confirm that these fish pay a lot of attention to what's happening above them. You'll usually see them looking at the spot where food is dropped down to them seconds later, as if they've seen signs of an imminent meal. In the wild, they react to movement above them too quickly to be taken with a cast net. (And I know; I've tried.) Apparently this reflex helps them feed on terrestrial prey.

I looked at the slowing ripples on the water and considered my Scum Frog. What I probably needed was a Scum Goldfinch.

Soon after the goldfinch incident, I cast my Scum Frog into a sweet spot where I was convinced there'd be a snakehead. A hit resulted immediately upon impact. I fought the moderate-sized fish and got a good look at it when it broke water. And then suddenly it was off and gone. I reeled in the Scum Frog and examined it. The legs were shredded but still attached.

I realized why I wasn't landing any snakeheads with the Scum Frog. The fish weren't swallowing it, as would a bass. They were biting the back legs and trying to tear them off to eat; they weren't getting hooked. I was only dragging them in for as long as they cared to clamp onto the rubber frog legs. The fish could let go whenever it wanted to.

By six o'clock, my whole body ached. I hadn't sat down or eaten in eleven hours. I figured I'd cast that fishing rod about a thousand times over the course of the day. Perhaps it was a blessing that by six thirty, I'd finally lost good old Scum Frog to that dangerous snag of a tree in the middle of the pond. Without the only lure that had worked at all, I was done for the day.

I came back early the next morning with an array of similar frog lures. Again I pounded the pond for hours on end, and again I had many strikes but hooked not a one. Running low on money for campgrounds and motels, I drove home to figure out how to land this challenging fish.

Unfortunately, as of this writing, I haven't managed to land a snakehead. I went back again and again all through the late summer and fall, camping up the road and spending my days casting for snakeheads until my wrists felt as if they would fall off. I saw plenty of them, and out of all the invasive species I hunted, I learned more about snakeheads through observation than I did about anything else, but they eluded me to the end.

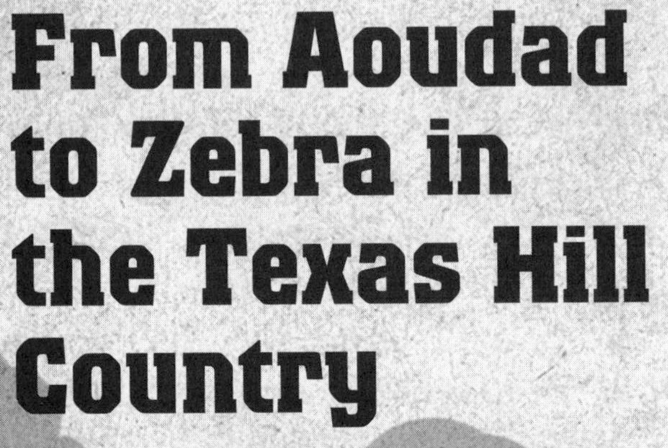

From Aoudad to Zebra in the Texas Hill Country

I KNEW I'D SPENT TOO MUCH TIME in the Hill Country of central Texas when we drove past a pair of dusty zebras standing by the side of the road and I didn't slow down to take a picture.

Willie Nelson's voice blared from the radio, and the car itself hummed beneath me as I downshifted around a corner, up a hill, past thickets of dying oaks and high fences and white limestone cliffs. It was the same car that had carried me thousands of miles around the country while I worked on this book — a little Ford ZX2 coupe, which I had usually piloted alone, with only the radio to talk to.

This time I had company. Helenah Swedberg, a documentary filmmaker, rode shotgun, keeping me awake and helping with directions. She'd found me through the Internet a few months earlier and started filming shortly thereafter. Many people have asked me to film documentaries or television pilots with them. Helenah, though, was unique: She'd gotten right on a train when I suggested we get to work rather than go back and forth with budgets and outlines and waiting for someone else's blessing for the project.

My trunk was packed with the usual guns, butchering tools, nets, fishing tackle, and camping gear. The backseat was heaped with Helenah's camera and sound equipment. I'm pretty good with a map, but I liked hearing the directions in a soft Swedish accent coming from a pretty blonde in the passenger seat.

I'd heard stories about hunting in Texas, particularly in the Hill Country. They were stories about enormous game ranches with almost every kind of animal you could imagine: African antelopes, such as kudu, impala, and sable. Strange Asian deer. Even rhinos, elephants, and lions. These are breeding populations of any animal to which a monetary or status value could be attached. If these animals were out there behind high fences for long enough, I thought, sooner or later a fence would get knocked down or a gate left open and animals would escape. For someone hunting invasive species, Texas could be Hell or the Promised Land, depending on how you look at it.

When I was offered a November residency for artists and writers on a large ranch between the towns of Kerr and Medina, I jumped on it. And when Helenah started following me everywhere with a camera, I suggested that she apply for the same residency in order to film on the ranch and to facilitate an epic road trip. Having someone to pay for half the gas was a nice angle, too.

We left Virginia as the leaves were changing, drove through the Deep South and the barbecue belt and along the Gulf Coast. The fall colors faded to green as we seemed to go backward in time. Somewhere in Mississippi the palm trees appeared and the barbecue joints became catfish houses and shacks with signs advertising boiled crawfish. Soon, we were in the Texas Hill Country, a part of the state suffering from what was shaping up to be a prolonged drought of historical proportions. Later in the trip, near San Antonio, I saw horses and cattle lying newly dead in their pastures, grim and emaciated. Fortunately, our host ranch possessed several natural springs and had more access to water than any other place I visited in the region.

The owners of the ranch had awarded me the residency based in large part on the work I was doing: creating awareness about invasive species. They'd been quoted in a newspaper article decrying the ecological and economic effects of the 2.6 million invasive pigs that plague Texas. Having hunted wild pigs, I was more interested in the other invasive species found in the Hill Country, such as aoudad, axis deer, and emu.

The Hill Country is, in a sense, one big private zoo. In the 1950s, a sort of fad developed when a rancher bought some excess aoudad from a public zoo and released them on his large, fenced property. Aoudad, also known as Barbary sheep, are native to the deserts of northern Africa and somewhat resemble bighorn sheep. They can survive without liquid water, getting all of their moisture from the plants that they eat: a ready-made survivor in dry country.

The aoudads reproduced quickly and were sold to neighboring ranchers as exotic pets and as big game for eventual hunting. Other species followed. In an area of families flush with oil money and sitting on enormous tracts of land, keeping the strangest game animals they could find was the new status symbol.

A few ranchers realized there might be some money in this. If people were willing to fly to Africa to hunt antelope, perhaps offering the same antelope to hunt closer to home would have appeal. The business of raising trophy-quality exotic game emerged. Raised either wholly wild or half-tame on big ranches, these animals became a cottage industry. Anything that a hunter would pay to go after was imported for this "sport."

Most landowners built high fences around their property; after all, nobody wanted to pay to stock impala if they were going to wander over to somebody else's land. Had the animals stayed put, maybe this scheme would have worked out. If there's one lesson to learn about invasive species, however, it's that wildlife doesn't want to stay put.

Our first morning in Texas, Helenah and I were looking for the ranch manager's house when we saw an axis deer — a species of spotted deer native to India — with a collar around its neck, standing in front of a tidy, one-story house. No fence confined it;

in fact, it walked over and sniffed my hand like it was a dog. (I was told later that the deer had been found as a fawn and bottle-raised by the ranch manager's children. Eventually, it mated with a passing wild axis buck and had fawns of its own.)

At first I was delighted by the opportunity to see and even touch an axis deer. But soon I realized that the fact these exotic deer were being kept as pets didn't bode well for my chances of hunting them.

Helenah and I caught up with Robert, the ranch manager, a cheerful, portly, mustachioed man in his fifties sporting an air of competence. When I asked him about aoudads and pigs, he told me the ranch owners had decided against my hunting for a while. A group of people who had paid to hunt on the property would arrive in a few days, and my hosts didn't want my shooting to spook the deer and pigs these people would be looking for.

This was a disappointment, but I understood the situation. I believed the owners' commitment to sound ecological practices: No high fences enclosed the property (allowing wildlife to freely cross boundaries, which has become the exception in much of Texas), and the fact that they raised bison rather than conventional cattle spoke to their willingness to encourage native species.

Because I didn't want to waste any time, I begged my hosts for one exception: that I be permitted to hunt invasive species on the ranch right away, but without the use of firearms. I would be on foot, armed only with a knife. They readily agreed.

Over the next few days, Helenah and I hiked and drove around the enormous ranch, gathering fossils, dodging bison, and filming material for her documentary. Herds of six to twenty wild pigs would emerge from thick cover and feed during the half hour before dusk. Whitetail deer were more plentiful on the ranch than anywhere else I've ever been. Now and then, I'd spot an Indian axis deer or a European fallow deer, easily distinguished from the native deer by the spotted coats of the adults.

My method of hunting began with me running after every group of pigs we saw. Usually at night, we'd be driving down one of the many dirt roads and spot the shapes of pigs in front of us or in a field. Helenah never got accustomed to my habit of suddenly stopping the car, jumping out, and running after a herd of pigs in the moonlight. Perhaps I could have been more diligent about setting the emergency brake before leaving her in the idling vehicle.

Sometimes I stalked them on foot before running for the final approach. Over the course of a week, I discovered several tricks to getting in close. A herd of fewer pigs was easier to stalk toward; there were fewer eyes to see me. The more ground I could cover by stalking rather than running, the better. Once I started sprinting at the pigs, they'd hear me, and when they began to run, it would all be over in less than thirty seconds. I needed to get to within twenty five yards (and preferably closer) or it was impossible to catch up with them before they'd make it into the woods. I could pursue them only in the open, as I'd lose sight of them in any sort of cover.

The use of slopes also proved key. If the pigs were even slightly uphill from me, I couldn't gain an inch of ground. On flat land, we were evenly matched. The ideal was to be running slightly (but not steeply) downhill at my prey.

I knew better than to try for a big one. Some of the pigs were well over three hundred pounds, and I stayed away from them. Without a pistol for backup, a boar or sow of that size could gore and bite me and possibly even kill me. I also wasn't going to touch any piglets, lest a large sow run over to defend her baby. My target, then, was a smallish pig between fifty and a hundred pounds, preferably toward the rear of the pack and without a really big pig next to it.

One night, shortly after dinner, Helenah looked out through the kitchen window and informed me that a herd of pigs was on the lawn. I sprang into action and ran out the door into the grunting, oinking herd.

My feet pounded the ground, and the sensation of a thorn poking into the sole of one foot brought home the fact that I had forgotten to put on shoes. Barefoot running is fine for some people, but a ranch dotted with piles of bison poop and thorny shrubs, in the dark, isn't the place for this kind of activity.

Nevertheless, I pressed on, encouraged that I was closer to getting a pig than ever before. I was only a few yards from a small one and could sense imminent victory. A few paces, and I could pounce on it and slip the long blade of my knife into the middle of the right shoulder, where lies the heart. My right hand went to my hip for the familiar feel of the hilt in its sheath and felt . . . nothing.

In the excitement of the moment, I had dashed from the cottage lacking not only my shoes but also my knife. It was still sitting on the kitchen counter, where I'd used it to chop vegetables.

I quickly had to acknowledge that there were a few boar in the herd big enough to do damage. As things stood, though, with me flying through the air in the moonlight, these animals were terrified of me. They had no idea that I couldn't defend myself against the tusks of even a medium-sized pig. To stop and turn around could be interpreted as a sign of weakness. I thought the best thing to do was to bluff and keep on chasing. I ran after them most of the way across the pasture through the short, stiff grass and the jimsonweed until they were well ahead of me. I was safe.

THE NEXT DAY, we went for a drive on the main road, toward Medina, to run some errands. At around noon, I was surprised to see several dozen deer grazing in the middle of a field. Whitetails don't normally venture into the open in the middle of the day. The color didn't look quite right for a whitetail, though, and there was a sort of horizontal band along the midsections. I slowed the car to get a better look and suddenly realized that I was looking at impala.

A herd of African antelope was living in the wild, right here in North America.

They were mostly females; a few had the distinctive horns grown only by males. They were of various sizes, and some were obviously this year's fawns. These impala were not captive livestock behind a high barrier: They were in a cow pasture with only a waist-high wire fence separating them from the road.

We drove back from Medina with eyes peeled and cameras out, on the alert for any other invasive animals. A dead, bloated axis deer lay by the side of the road. We passed a couple of aoudads on a neighboring ranch. While we were bouncing down a dirt road, a European fallow deer ran out in front of the car. Panicked, it tried to escape by running more than a hundred yards beside the road, along a low fence that any native whitetail would have bounded over. It came to an open gate, skidded to a halt, and stared at it for several seconds before realizing that it could run through it and get away. Perhaps this is one reason why the whitetails still dominate the landscape and the axis and fallow deer are fewer in number; the whitetails are just a bit smarter. It was the pair of grazing zebras that made me realize how bizarre the invasive species situation is in Texas. Helenah was not impressed by them, having spent several months studying and traveling in Africa. But to me, nothing says "exotic" like a zebra.

The severe lack of rain was ravaging Central Texas. The epic drought was devastating to ranchers and livestock alike. The price of a bale of hay had more than tripled over the year, if you could even find one for sale. Many ranch owners resorted to trucking it in from as far away as Louisiana and Mississippi to keep their herds alive. I saw an alarming number of hay trucks heading west on I-10 on both ends of my trip, but not everyone could afford to transport what became a rare commodity.

Aside from trucking in food, there were few options open to livestock owners. As the grass dried up and the animals lost weight, many could do nothing but watch them die. Others sold them for slaughter. These were the choices for people raising cattle; for those with exotic animals on their land, the situation was even more dire.

It's not easy getting a band of impalas or a couple of wild zebras to step into the back of a livestock truck to be taken to a slaughterhouse. Even if you could, what was the market for zebra meat? These animals were not tame. They lived on ranches of thousands of acres in a more or less wild state, though there were artificial feeders strategically placed.

A few locals told me in confidence that some ranchers were quietly opening the gates and letting the exotic species leave. If there wasn't enough forage on their property, the reasoning went, perhaps the animals could manage to survive somewhere else. Even valuable trophy animals stocked for "canned hunts" were released. Also, the ongoing economic downturn meant not many people were willing to shell out thousands of dollars to shoot a cape buffalo or a wildebeest.

It's difficult to gauge how much of a problem exists now, a year later, in terms of species diversity and quantity (aside from the wild hogs, which have been studied in some depth). Not all of these species will become invasive; they're competing with native wildlife adapted to the habitat. In twenty years, the zebras and axis deer may or may not still be around. But some of the African imports have a good chance, not just of surviving but of expanding their range as well. Many come from arid conditions and could do quite well in a drought.

At last the paying hunters left the ranch, and finally I could have my opportunity. I met with Robert again to discuss house rules. I told him I was interested in hunting and eating aoudad, axis deer, sika, emu, and perhaps some pigs. In deference to my hosts, though, I explained that whatever species was causing the most problems could be my target.

Robert made a face and looked down.

"We leave those sika deer alone. They like to feed them up by the main house."

"How about the aoudad and axis deer?"

"The aoudad are off-limits. The axis deer are, too, but you won't see all that many of them; most of them left for good when we let them out."

"Let them out?" I was puzzled.

"A few years ago, we brought some and kept them in a big enclosure for a while so they'd get used to the place, but when we let them out, they mostly wandered off the ranch."

I was dumbfounded. These kind, intelligent people had deliberately brought in an exotic species and released it into the wild. As a guest, I was grateful to them for inviting me to the ranch. I liked Robert, and everyone else who kept the ranch running. Reconciling my respect for him with the deliberate release of axis deer was difficult.

"The pigs are okay, though," he said. "We talked about it and it's okay for you to take a pig."

"Wait a minute. Didn't you guys want the pigs gone? I have them pretty well patterned, and I could probably take three or four at a time with a rifle before the herd gets away."

"Well," said Robert, "we've got this other group coming in a few weeks, and we don't want them spooked."

That's when the real human aspect of the problem in Texas sank in. The people coming to hunt were paying seventeen hundred dollars apiece to stay at the ranch for a multiday pig-hunting program, with catered meals to boot. No pigs would mean no customers. Despite the ecological damage wild hogs cause, at the end of the day, the ranchers needed them.

For the next few days I stared in frustration at strange quadrupeds from around the world that I wasn't permitted to pursue. Helenah and I saw a few more antelope, probably impalas or blackbucks. I watched a European red stag behind a fence down the road. I had stumbled into the invasivore's Shangri-La, only to find that most of the menu was off-limits.

I GOT MY PIG, but it took a while.

Most hunting in Texas is done from large, elevated box blinds. Imagine a wooden or metal box with a narrow window on each side and a door in the back. The biggest window faces an aluminum feeder that automatically sprays out corn twice a day.

To the ranchers who erect these blinds and feeders, much of the satisfaction of the hunt takes place before it begins. They may stock the property with the offspring of trophy animals to improve the genetics. They spend years watching to see which bucks are developing better than others. They plant food plots and experiment with feed mixtures. It's like playing Farmville with wild animals, except with real science and real skill.

To a visitor, that work is invisible. Although I don't believe it's possible to cheat at hunting when you're doing it to put meat on the table or to help an ecosystem in trouble, I couldn't stomach the idea of hunting from a box blind. I don't foist my views about fair play on others, but for me, the box blind isn't sporting.

Instead, I found an open area with plenty of fresh tracks and pig poop, with clear trails to it from a wooded hill above. Checking the wind, I moved a hundred and thirty yards downwind and sat behind some fallen branches as natural cover. Helenah sat just behind me with her camera.

We waited for a long time as the sun dropped below hills covered with live oaks. Strange noises came from the woods and coyotes howled. A chill moved in and the light turned gray in the last minutes before dark. A crashing sound from the hillside told us the pigs had come. The herd filed into the open. When I lifted my bolt action .30-'06, I could barely make out the big sow in the scope's crosshairs as I squeezed the trigger.

The dead pig, with its black body clad with stiff dark bristles, looked like one of the Eurasian wild strains that are referred to in the U.S. as a Russian razorback, a breed not often raised on farms. This pig's ancestors must have been put out here on purpose.

The pig was too heavy to move; besides, I wasn't going to put a pig carcass in my compact car. I butchered it there in the field under the headlights of my car. I crammed the meat into a large cooler, which we hoisted into the backseat, then headed back to the cottage for ice.

We rolled to a stop before fording a small stream that crossed the road. Suddenly, we heard splashing through the open windows. Some sort of animal, between the size of a deer and an elk, was walking rapidly along the stream, crossing the road from our right to the left. It had long, wide palmate antlers, like those of a moose, and was very dark. Whatever it was, it definitely wasn't a Texas native. I had no idea what it was, and I still don't. I can't even guess which continent it came from.

WITH A COOLER FULL OF PORK, I didn't know what to do with myself for the remainder of my residency. Without Internet access, it was difficult to finish the research and writing I'd intended to do. I realized the next morning that I couldn't bear to see the global menagerie of invasive meat running around and not be able to do anything about it. It was time to go home.

The Hill Country is an easy landscape to fall in love with. There's romance in knowing you could walk around the corner and find yourself face to face with anything from an antelope to a zebra. I liked everything about Texas: the food, the radio stations, and especially the people. Their relationship with exotic wildlife is probably a disaster unfolding in slow motion, but it's exciting and fascinating nonetheless.

The pork was delicious, perhaps because acorns, which pigs love, had been thick on the ground. Even a ham I brined and smoked hurriedly had a texture, a color, and a richness of flavor like no other pork I'd ever eaten. Then again, perhaps the pork was good simply because I had worked hard for it and butchered it by my own hand.

Chinese Mystery Snails

OCCASIONALLY DURING THE COURSE OF MY HUNTS, I stumbled across invasive species I wasn't looking for. One afternoon, I was walking around a pond looking for Canada geese to photograph for a blog entry. I didn't find any, but I did see what looked like enormous spiral seashells scattered along the shore. I couldn't think of any native snails that got this big: The shells were up to three inches long, and very dark in color. I slipped a few into my pocket.

Back home, I did some research. I quickly concluded that I was looking at Chinese mystery snails, *Bellamya chinensis*. These mollusks are Asian natives often found in the aquarium trade in this country. They're omnivorous feeders — almost any aquatic plant available might be on the menu, and they'll devour rotting debris, too. This is why hobbyists like them so much: They help keep a fish tank or a koi pond free of algae and left-over fish food.

From my research, I learned that these snails were introduced into the wild, among other ways, when Lake Erie was stocked with them in the 1940s, with the idea that the snails would provide good forage for flathead catfish. What happened is that the catfish weren't especially interested in them. This might be just as well, as the catfish themselves were part of a long parade of nonnative species that humans stocked in the Great Lakes.

It's difficult to say exactly what effect the Chinese mystery snails had on Lake Erie. It had been an ecological mess long before their introduction, from pollution and overfishing. And sorting out the damage from one species of snail amid the damage from introductions of smelt, brown trout, alewife, perch, common carp, rainbow trout, and coho salmon is too complicated.

What we know for sure is that when Chinese mystery snails make an appearance, native species of snails decline to irrelevance or disappear altogether. In their native China, these snails must have an array of natural predators. (Unfortunately, scant research has been conducted on them, even in their natural environment.) In North America, no predator seems to fancy them, so once they become established, they're difficult to eradicate.

Once I knew what to look for, I began seeing mystery snails in other places. When I went fishing for invasive snakehead fish along the Potomac River, I saw along the shore mystery snails by the thousands. A park service naturalist told me they'd shown up a few years earlier and quickly dominated the shallows. First, they expanded their numbers, no doubt displacing native fauna. Then, once it seemed like the river couldn't possibly pack in any more invasive snails per square foot, in summer 2010 the temperature spiked and stayed high for months. The species apparently has trouble with rapid temperature changes. The result was a shoreline ruined for weeks by the stench of rotting snail carcasses. There were enough survivors in deeper water, however, that within a year the population was on the rebound.

Temperature changes like the one in 2010 could eventually wipe out the Chinese mystery snail in many parts of its introduced range. Indeed, many invasive species could succumb in this way, wiped out by an unusually cold winter or a blistering summer. Green iguanas, for example, are still a big problem in the Florida Keys and in parts of southern Florida, but they were once a threat as far north as Sarasota. Then, along came the winter of 2009, and its extended deep freeze decimated the more northerly population. Green iguanas don't retreat into burrows, the way black spiny-tailed iguanas do, and thus have no protection against prolonged bouts of cold weather. For a while, they go into a state of torpor, meaning their metabolism slows dramatically. In this condition, they're unable to move or escape predation. If the temperature rises soon enough, they'll recover; if not, they die.

North America is subject to broad swings in temperatures; maybe the Chinese mystery snails won't make it here in the long run. Who knows if they'll be present in a hundred years? The trouble is that it won't take a hundred years for them to eat many native North American species into extinction. Imagine what would happen if they destroyed all the native snails from a number of river systems and then in twenty years themselves died out during a heat spell. We'd be left with no snails at all, with the cascading effects throughout the ecosystem that would result from a buildup of aquatic detritus.

After I came upon that first population of invasive snails, I started making phone calls. First, I got in touch with the owner of the pond. That happened to be the Thomas Jefferson Foundation, which owns and operates Monticello, the estate of our third president.

The irony hit me immediately: Thomas Jefferson was an architect, engineer, and philosopher — and a plant hunter. In his pursuit of horticulture, he experimented with growing many exotic plants here in Virginia. The most notorious locally is the tree of paradise, which is now a much-hated roadside weed. It thrives in disturbed land and is known for burrowing its roots into house foundations and for invading hay fields. A nursery owner in New York first imported the plant into the United States in the 1790s, but it was the author of the Declaration of Independence who brought it to Virginia. And now, less than a mile from Monticello, on land owned by the foundation bearing his name, another invasive species had gotten a foothold.

I met with the gentleman in charge of that section of the grounds. As we strolled around the pond, he explained how the snails appeared and became more and more numerous, eventually crunching underfoot with every step as volunteers walked around to maintain the gardens.

He was somewhat sympathetic, though unconcerned about the ecological consequences of allowing Chinese mystery snails to escape into the river that feeds into the Chesapeake Bay, claiming it wasn't his problem. He said the foundation would be willing to allow removal of the snails if Virginia's Department of Game and Inland Fisheries would give the matter its blessing. Fair enough.

My next step was to talk with the district biologist for the Department of Game and Inland Fisheries, Mike Dye. Mike had always been of great help when I needed something from his organization, and now he put me in touch with one of the department's aquatic biologists. Through e-mail, that person asked me to bring him some samples of the snails in question. I rounded up half a dozen snails of various sizes in sample jars filled with rubbing alcohol and delivered them to his office. And then I waited.

At first I wasn't worried; it was fall, and the snails would be going dormant for the winter. (In warm weather, they reproduce prolifically, so that's when they must be kept in check. I discovered this when I put two of them in a small aquarium and tallied up their offspring daily for two months. Within a month, my initial pair had turned into close to forty.) Anyway, the cold months ahead lulled me into thinking we had plenty of time.

I also tried my hand at cooking Chinese mystery snails. Culturally, Westerners have some context for eating snails; most of us are familiar with the role of another species of snail (*Helix pomatia,* better known as the Burgundy snail) in French cuisine.

It didn't seem a huge stretch, then, to eat Chinese mystery snails. In fact, there have been large-scale attempts at farming them as an inexpensive substitute for the French snails.

I have tasted Chinese mystery snails cooked side-by-side with Burgundy snails in otherwise identical recipes, as an experiment with chef Brian Helleberg at his Charlottesville, Virginia, restaurant, Fleurie (which specializes in traditional French cuisine). Brian was not impressed with the Chinese snails because their texture simply does not compare well to the silky smoothness of well-handled Burgundy snails. I agree with him that real French snails are much better — in French cuisine. The Chinese snails are not going to be a viable substitute for the only snails we are accustomed to eating. Their flavor is similar (rather bland, tasting mostly like whatever they are cooked with).

However, I think that Chinese mystery snails are a lot like some other mollusks that we're all used to eating. They remind me a lot of slightly rubbery New England–style fried clams or of fake scallops. These snails aren't going to be four-star cuisine, but after being tenderized, fried, and served with tartar sauce, they're quite good.

When spring rolled around, nothing had happened. I had no report from the DGIF and no authorization from the Thomas Jefferson Foundation to kill the snails there. I e-mailed the aquatic biologist; no reply.

In early August, I spoke on the phone with a game warden and had what seemed like a good discussion about the situation. He thought the aquatic biologist had retired, and said he'd have someone else call me back. I never heard from anyone. It is disheartening, but I try to bear in mind that nobody has given any of these people a budget or a mandate to deal with this problem. Individually, they're all doing their best, I'm sure. They have their own universes of routines and problems to deal with. The idea that we all need to start paying attention to some snail is probably the last thing they want to think about.

To date, nothing official has happened as a result of my reporting this infestation. I heard from Monticello employees that someone had been keen on donating an aquarium full of fish and snails but had been turned down. The pond is right off the road and is an easy offloading point for anyone looking to dump an aquarium. The really big question is, What, exactly, had that tank contained? A stream drains that pond into the larger watershed. As I write, I have little doubt that invasive snails are working their way into that watershed and toward the Chesapeake Bay.

Less than a week after my fruitless conversation with the game warden, I was fishing in a reservoir near the James River. I was alone, a fishing rod in my right hand and a five-gallon bucket in my left hand, walking down the dam's spillway, and happened to look down into a pool of running water. Sadly, what I saw were those familiar spiral, three-inch-long shells. Chinese mystery snails.

I carefully set the fishing rod on the smooth gray rocks. I rolled up my jeans, stepped into the frigid water, and began picking up snails, dropping them into my bucket one by one.

After

word

The Ones That Got Away

THROUGHOUT THE COURSE of working on this book, there were a lot of hunts that didn't pan out. Some of what I'd expected to be the easiest species to bag turned out to be the most difficult.

I thought pigeons and starlings would be a breeze; both species are rampant in just about every city in America. As I discovered, though, *ubiquitous* doesn't mean "easy to hunt." In every metropolis this side of the Khyber Pass, it's frowned upon to discharge firearms within city limits. I can't disagree with this view, but it definitely makes hunting awkward. If I could have used a pellet gun, I'd have been successful.

The first invasive species I hunted was starlings. When you look into the American sky and see a flock of tens of thousands of birds, moving together in an undulating mass like a single life-form, those are starlings. There are more of them in North America than any other bird since the heyday of the passenger pigeon.

These starlings came here in the early 1890s, the result of several introductions orchestrated by a New York City organization called the American Acclimatization Society. Eugene Schieffelin, a pharmacist by trade, for several years was president of the group. It's said that Schieffelin's goal was to introduce into New York City every species of bird mentioned in the works of Shakespeare.

I really want to believe this story because it's romantic, but I haven't been able to find a primary source confirming it. Regardless of motive, it's a matter of record that the AAS brought the beloved English starling (along with many other bird species) to New York City.

The starling has some advantages over many native American songbirds. First, it's not picky about its diet and is quite content to eat insects, seeds, and anything else well-meaning people offer. Second, it thrives in a variety of habitats. Third, it's a good fighter. As a cavity nester — unlike, say, the robin, which nests on tree branches — it requires a hollow cavity in which to build its nest. Although it has competition for this scarce commodity in the native purple martins, bluebirds, and yellow-bellied sapsuckers, a starling is usually victorious in battle.

Equally important is the bird's prolific production of eggs. Most native songbirds produce one clutch of young per year; a starling will bring off clutch after clutch of eggs. Whereas a bluebird raises three or four young in a year, a starling may raise eight to ten. Over time, this gives starlings a huge advantage in scrambling among species for nesting sites, diminishing habitat, and food.

Seeing how the black, iridescent birds with back-swept wings congregate in massive flocks, I decided to hunt them on my rural property in central Virginia. The challenge was the sheer size of their flock; starlings by the thousands would pass high over my land. Any sort of wing-shooting with a shotgun amounts to picking out a target and "leading" it — that is, swinging ahead of it and squeezing the trigger before the bird arrives, as it takes time for the lead shot to travel to a particular spot in midair. I'd had plenty of practice with mourning doves and Canada geese, so I thought I knew what I was doing. The staggering number of starlings, however, made that tactic moot.

There were so many birds that I couldn't keep track of one long enough to lead it and squeeze off a shot. I would begin well enough, then not be sure which bird I was looking at, then think of shooting anyhow (forgetting that a flock consists not just of birds but of space between them as well). By the time I decided to shoot, that mass of birds was out of range.

Later, in contemplating what had happened, I came to understand a significant advantage afforded to any creature that's part of a flock, a school, or a herd. A major challenge of hunting animals living in such a group is not a matter of speed or cunning: It's being able to select one prey and keep track of it.

I heard an account of a leopard in Africa that entered a barn and sauntered past pens filled with immobile goats in order to take one particular animal, farther back and not as convenient. The leopard went out of its way in pursuit of this one.

Likewise, there are many videos of lions and cheetahs passing slower animals because they were fixated, for some reason, on one animal. They do this because they must. If a hunter switches suddenly to another target because it's slower, it follows that he'll switch to one that's even slower, then another, until suddenly the entire herd is gone and the hunter is left with nothing. One of the most important skills of a subsistence hunter is to pick a target and let everything else fall away.

I spent dozens of hours in the middle of the field in front of my house, trying to swing on to a high and fast starling, failing, left with nothing and without having pulled the trigger. Often a neighbor pulled up in front of his house, got out of his car, looked over at me, and shook his head.

It was as if the starlings were taunting me. I saw hundreds of them in Charlottesville, Virginia, a short drive from my home. I'd watch them, at times no more than a dozen feet away, but I was legally forbidden to shoot them. I still feel itchy and restless when I see a starling close by.

Pigeons were a similar conundrum. Ubiquitous and even more urban than starlings, the rock dove hails from Europe (where, like in many other places around the world, it's raised for food) and was brought to North America during early colonial times.

Although you'll see pigeons scavenging on farms and anywhere else large amounts of grain are stored, most people associate them with cities. I tried hunting them in both situations, but the ideal place for a pigeon hunt for me was New York City. The idea of hunting and eating Big Apple pigeons was tempting; the species is so common there that I thought it would be a cinch to get some.

With a speaking engagement in the city approaching, I decided to build a pigeon trap that I could place on a friend's rooftop. The design constraint was that I had to be able to fit it into a piece of airline-approved luggage. To accommodate this, I would build a box-type trap that could be broken down into six hinged panels that would fit into my suitcase.

I stood in the aisle of the hardware store, rubbing my chin, and staring at various pieces of brass hardware. An employee approached to ask what I was looking for and whether I needed assistance.

"Well, I'm building a trap. A box-type thing. It needs to break down and fit in my suitcase," I explained, somewhat absentmindedly.

The red-vested employee nodded, with a look on his face that indicated anything but comprehension.

"It has to get past TSA. And go back together easily. And stay shut properly. You know, for the kill."

The clerk disappeared, fast.

A week later I was in Manhattan with the friend on the roof of his apartment building, screwing together the panels of my pigeon trap. We baited it with bread crumbs, and all he had to do was pull the string when pigeons were in it.

In retrospect, my mistake was building a trap that caught the pigeons live rather than killing them automatically. It was unfair of me to expect a regular city-dweller to open the lid, grab a pigeon, and break its neck. My friend told me that, despite the disappearance of the crumbs, there were never any pigeons in the trap. Killing something in so personal a way is not easy to do.

Later attempts at taking urban pigeons were similarly doomed. In Charlottesville, I tried to throw my cast net over one for dinner. There were plenty of pigeons, but they were usually too high for the net (with a pellet gun, they'd have been goners). On other occasions, in a park, for example, and again with the net, there were pigeons but also small children watching. That was that. . . .

Once I organized a proper expedition on a large parcel of public land reported to harbor massive numbers of starlings and a moderate amount of pigeons. It was even planted with a grain crop. It should have been a slam-dunk. I brought along several former students from deer-hunting classes, as well as my father-in-law, Bob, my brother, a few other friends, and a producer for National Public Radio.

This substantial bunch of hunters I'd gathered spent the day sitting at the edge of a field doing absolutely nothing. It was utterly mortifying. We were doing everything right, except the birds failed to show up. One fellow, an alumnus of one of my hunting classes, said he saw a few starlings that flew away before he could get off a shot. I suspect he was just trying to make me feel better about the terrible location I'd chosen.

These two species were supposed to be my easiest targets, yet I failed in all my attempts to take them. I learned two things, though. First, sometimes there's a reason why an invasive species is successful. If it was easy to kill, maybe it would be gone already. Second, it's usually the rules and restrictions imposed by humans that enable an invasive species to thrive.

These local failures are painful to confess, considering I went to such great lengths to collect invasive lionfish and nutria. Many times I could have grabbed a pigeon out of the air beside a subway entrance in Manhattan or Paris. Just as often, though, I probably would've been mobbed by incensed locals calling for the police (or the gendarmes).